CANDYLUST

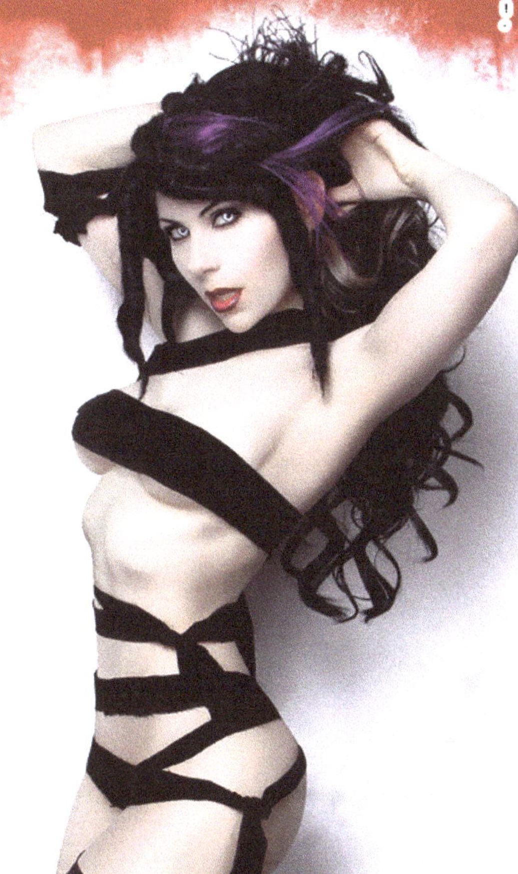

NEW YORK BASED PHOTOGRAPHY
SPECIALIZING IN

GOTHIC, FASHION, BEAUTY, FETISH, PIN UP, & BAND PHOTOGRAPHY

CANDYLUST.ORG

CANDYLUST_PHOTO@HOTMAIL.COM

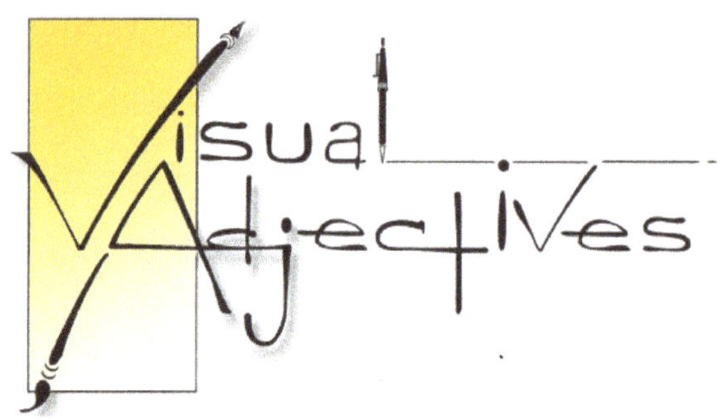

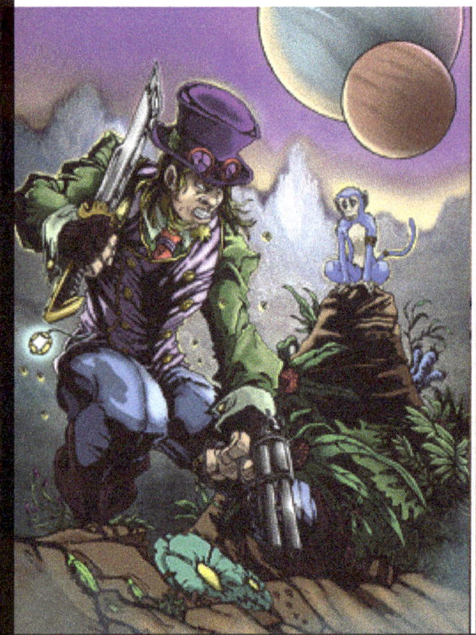

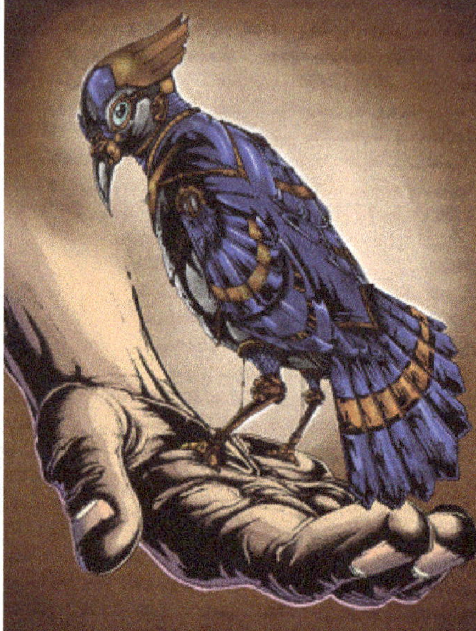

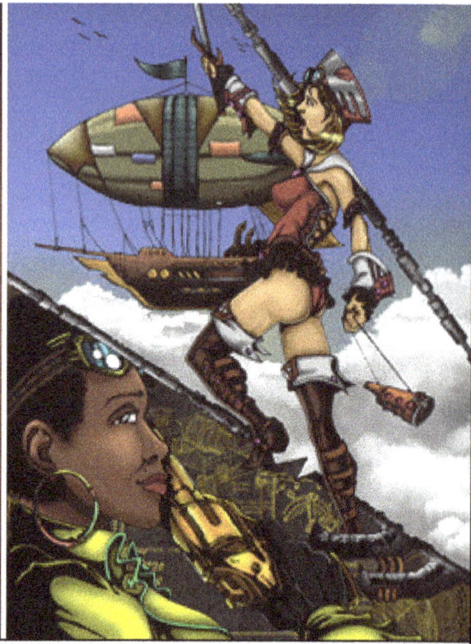

| Mercenary Edition | Engineer Edition | Captain Edition |

Visual Adjectives presents

NEW LEGENDS: MERCENARY • ENGINEER • CAPTAIN
a **Steampunk Anthology**.

With a wide variety of authors introducing their fantastic and innovative ideas into a collection of Steampunk short stories. Visual Adjectives offers a fresh take on one of the fastest growing genres and cultures!

With artwork done by "in-house" talents,
NEW LEGENDS: MERCENARY • ENGINEER • CAPTAIN
is the accumulated work of dedication and creativity.

For more information visit: **www.visualadjectives.com**
or send an email to **info@visadj.com** if you have any questions about being an author in the next anthology.

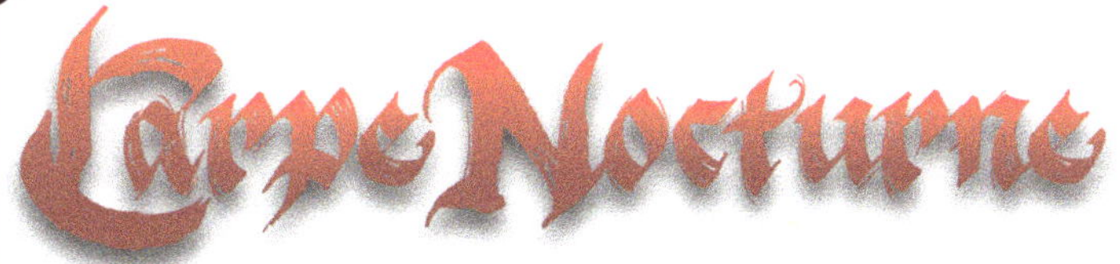

ARTS

ENTERTAINMENT

FASHION

FILM AND LITERATURE

INTERVIEWS

LIFE AND STYLE

MUSIC

REVIEWS

TECHNOLOGY

Carpe Nocturne Magazine
Volume 9 · Fall Issue
is a publication of Visual Adjectives, LLC and published four times a year.
All reviews and coverage expressed in this publication are the opinions of the writer
and/or those being interviewed and may not be shared by Visual Adjectives.
Copyright © 2014 by Visual Adjectives, LLC.
14280 Military Trail, #7501, Delray Beach, FL 33482, USA.
All rights reserved. No work may be copied or reproduced without the express
permission of the editor or publisher.
Correspondence should be addressed to:
Visual Adjectives
ATTN: Publisher, Carpe Nocturne Magazine
14280 Military Trail, #7501, Delray Beach, FL 33482, USA.
E-mail: editor@carpenocturnemagazine.com
www.carpenocturnemagazine.com
561-809-3834.

SUBSCRIBE AND SAVE

Name *(Print)*

Address 1 *(Print)*

Address 2 *(Print)*

City/State/Zip *(Print)*

Phone *(Print)*

Special Offer SAVE NOW ON Digital and Print Edition!

❑ Digital $5.00
❑ Print $20.00
❑ Print and Digital $24.00

❑ Bill me!
❑ Check/money order enclosed.

Charge: ❑MC ❑Visa ❑Amex ❑Disc

Card# *(Print)*

Exp. Date *(Print)*

Signature
You will be contacted before processing.

❑ **Yes, I would like to sign up for your monthly newletter.**

Email *(Print)*

Carpe Nocturne Magazine
ATTN: Subscribe
14280 Military Trail, #7501
Delray Beach, FL 33482

Carpe Nocturne is published 4 times a year. The cover price is $6.95. Canada add $9 per year, all other countries $15 per year. Must be paid in U.S. funds.

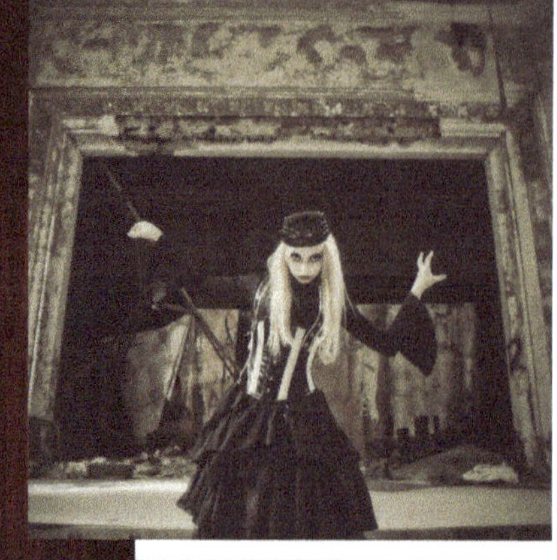

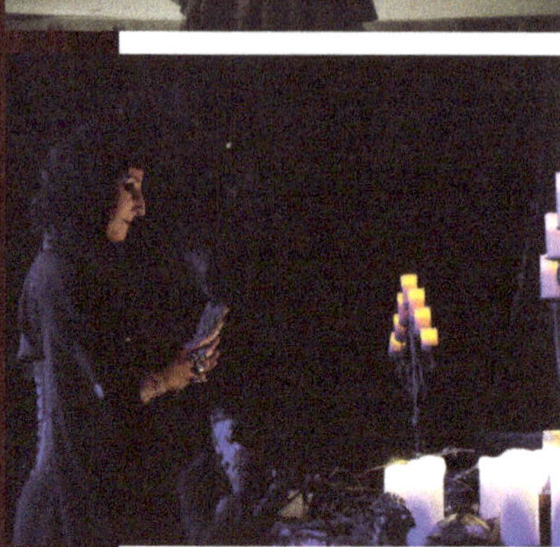

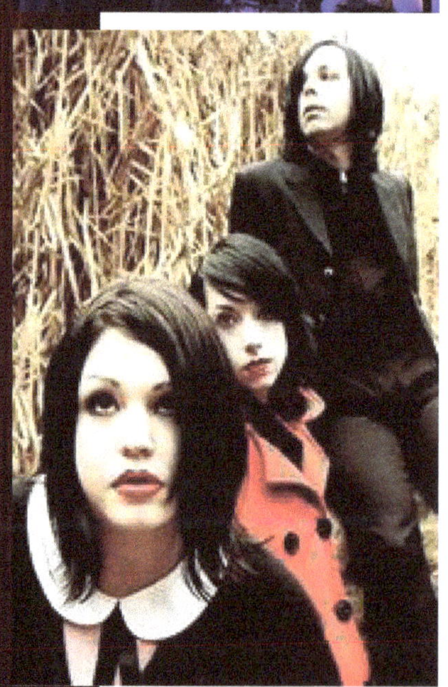

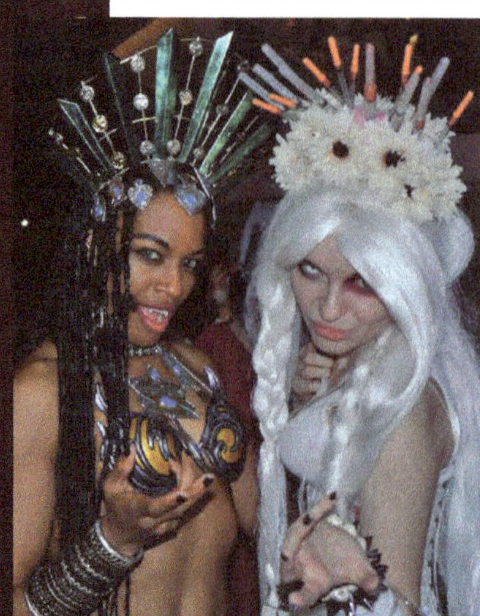

FEATURES

REGULARS

LIFE AND STYLE

ENTERTAINMENT

FROM THE EDITOR

I love Halloween. I know that sounds cliché coming from a magazine that tends to spend a lot of time covering the Goth scene, but it's true. I love Halloween for many of the reasons most fans of the holiday do, but a major factor in my affection for the tradition has to do with the season itself. See, down here in hot and grimy South Florida we take what seasonal changes we can get with enthusiasm. Autumn isn't so much autumn for us as it is a Summer-With-A-Slight-Breeze-That-Lasts-For-One-Weekend-In-October. Yet, that slight, near non-existent lick of air is enough to reinvigorate my senses and fill me with anticipation for what is to come.

Fall often symbolizes change, and anyone turning the pages in this issue of Carpe Nocturne can easily see that a lot has changed in a very short amount of time. Change can be both a scary and encouraging concept. My hope is that the recent transition isn't too jarring, and more than that, I hope that we are able to make Carpe Nocturne more accessible to our readership. We want this to remain the same magazine, with the same writers, same contributors and the same interests that made Carpe Nocturne what it is to begin with.

We also want to expand on our content and include more reporting on the darker literary genres. Expect to see more horror, sci-fi and fantasy with future issues. Carpe Nocturne will also, for the very first time be made available for print on demand. My goal is to increase the availability of our quarterly issues. One day I hope to see Carpe Nocturne grace the tablet screens and coffee tables of every dark culture enthusiast.

Finally, more than anything, I hope to hear from you. Carpe Nocturne is still your space and no one knows it better than you do. What needs to be improved? Which parts are a welcome change? Send any and all your comments, concerns and suggestions to comments@ carpenocturne.net, or drop us a line on our Facebook and Twitter pages. In the meantime, enjoy the Fall issue!

Annabella Rios,
Layout and Design

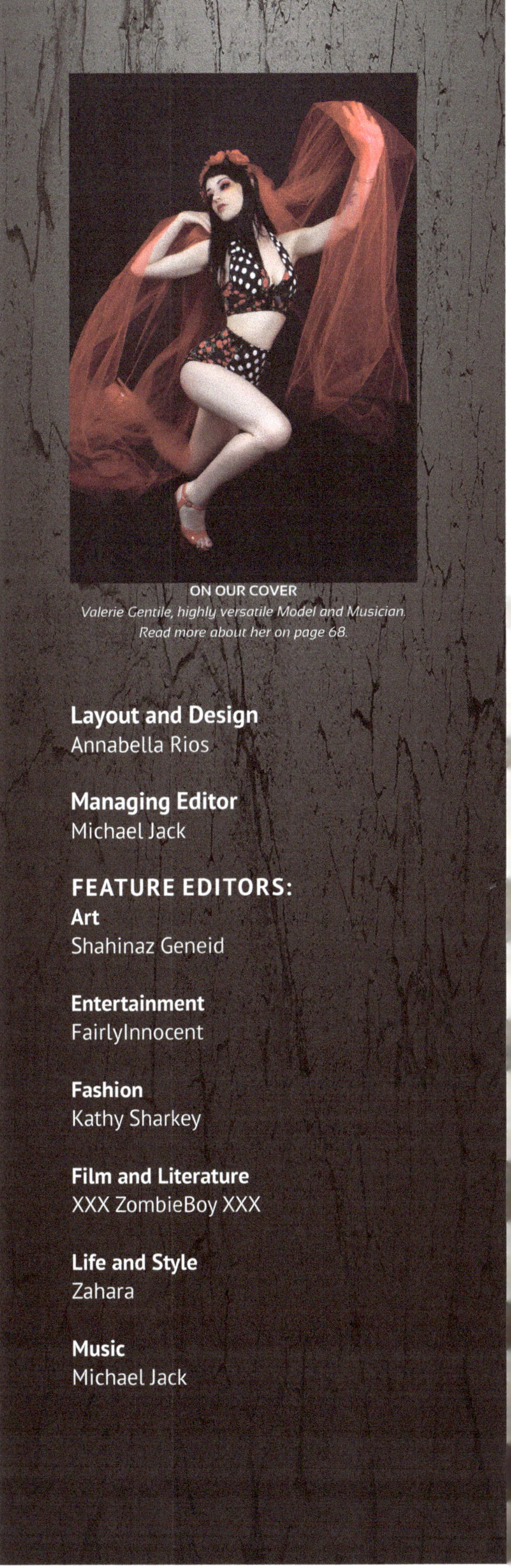

ON OUR COVER
Valerie Gentile, highly versatile Model and Musician.
Read more about her on page 68.

Layout and Design
Annabella Rios

Managing Editor
Michael Jack

FEATURE EDITORS:
Art
Shahinaz Geneid

Entertainment
FairlyInnocent

Fashion
Kathy Sharkey

Film and Literature
XXX ZombieBoy XXX

Life and Style
Zahara

Music
Michael Jack

CARPE NOCTURNE MAGAZINE
ADVERTISING
Display Ad Prices & Specs

Carpe Nocturne Magazine offers great marketing solutions for your business while reaching readers worldwide. Let us help you promote your business and events. Advertise in Carpe Nocturne Magazine and target individuals who participate in and share the creative view of all things Fantasy, Gothic, Sci-Fi, and Steampunk.

Advertising inside Carpe Nocturne Magazine is a cost effective way to promote your business, service or online shop to an international audience. We have readers in over 48 countries and over 20,000 hit on our website per month. Copies are distributed to readers quarterly and our distribution expands exponentially with each issue.

Carpe Nocturne Magazine is an independent, high impact publication. Our appeal is being a niche publication that is greatly coveted by readers. Our focus and the sense of community we create goes a long way, and the impressions we make are shared by loyal readers with common interests.

Let Carpe Nocturne Magazine help you reach your target market and be part of an environment that complements what you are advertising.

Prominently placed Web Site Banners (with links) are available for the home page and interior pages.

All ads appear in both digital and print editions of the magazine. All ads are in color.
Please send all ads and ad-related questions to: ads@carpenocturne.net

WEB SITE BANNER ADVERTISEMENTS

Homepage Full Banner	468px X 60px
Single Page Full Banner	468px X 60px
Right Sidebar Medium Rectangle	300px x 250px
Right Sidebar Verticle Rectangle	240px x 400px
Right Sidebar Verticle Banner	120px x 240px
Right Sidebar Rectangle	180px x 150px
Square Button	

2014 TO 2015 QUARTERLY ADVERTISING DEADLINE

ISSUE	PAYMENT DUE	ADS DUE	PUBLISHED DATE
Winter 2015	November 1, 2014	November 15, 2014	January 15, 2015
Spring 2015	February 1, 2015	February 15, 2015	April 15, 2015
Summer 2015	May 1, 2015	May 15, 2015	July 15, 2015
Fall 2015	August 1, 2015	August 15, 2015	October 15, 2015

Ads received after the deadline may be considered for use in the following issue, space permitting.

Carpe Nocturne Magazine
ATTN: Advertising
14280 Military Trail, #7501
Delray Beach, FL 33482

Questions? Email us at ads@carpenocturne.net

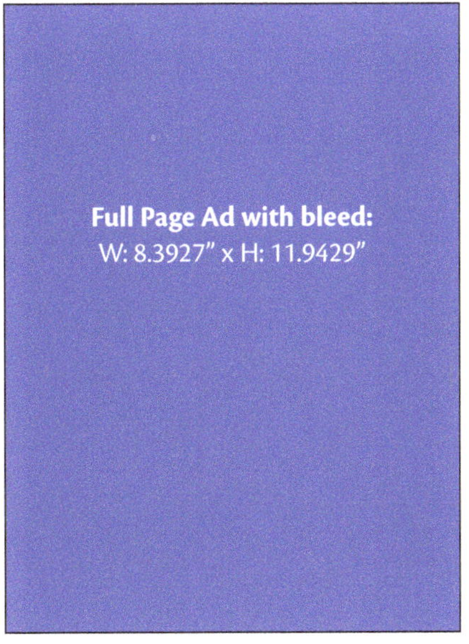

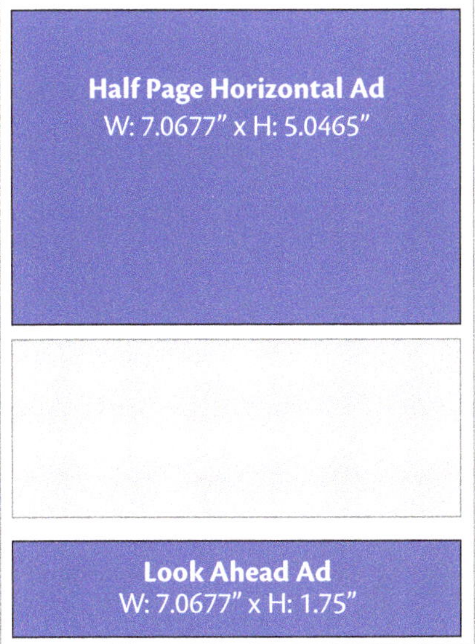

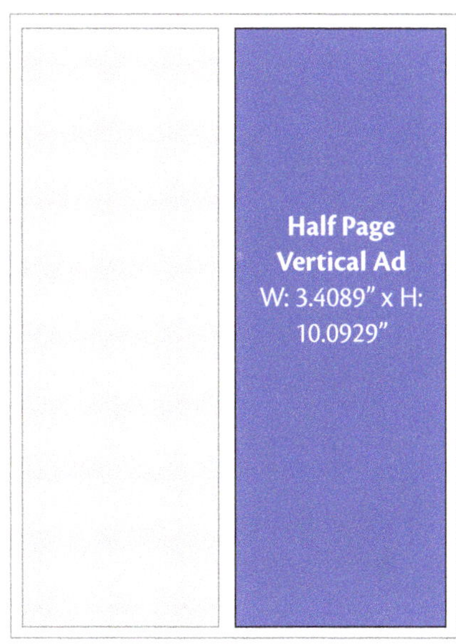

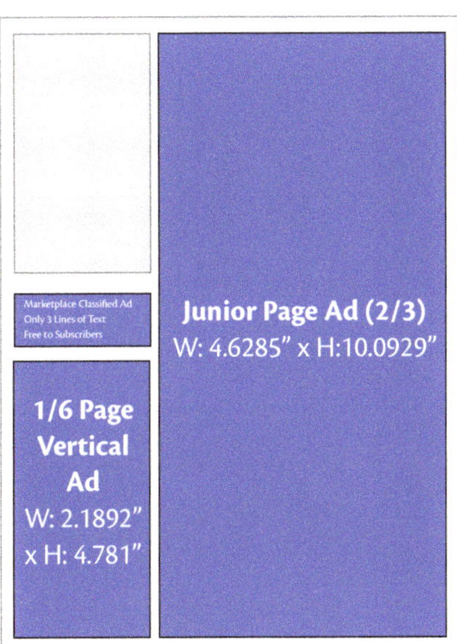

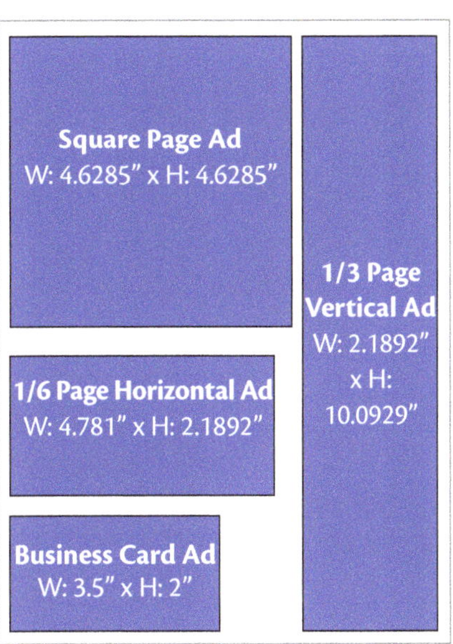

FREE IS FREE

PLACE A CLASSIFIED AD IF THE ITEM IS FREE THE AD IS FREE

AD TYPES
BACK COVER
FULL PAGE
JUNIOR PAGE (2/3)
HALF PAGE
SQUARE PAGE
1/3 PAGE
1/6 PAGE
LOOK AHEAD
BUSINESS CARD
MARKETPLACE CLASSIFIED

GUIDELINES

All ads must be submitted as high-resolution (press quality) format.
The resolution of all images must be supplied in 300dpi at 100%.
File types include .JPG, .EPS, .PSD, .AI, TIFF, GIF, or .PDF.
Ads may be submitted by: e-mail, submission manager, or postal mail on disc.
All fonts/typefaces must be embedded in PDF files.
The total file size of attachments in one e-mail must not exceed 5MB.
FTP site to upload larger file sizes is available on request.
Always include your name, your business/service name in all correspondence.
If you are unable to supply complete digital artwork to our specifications,
our Art Department can produce artwork at a subsidized charge.
Payment must be paid in full before the ad will be printed.
We are not responsible for errors due to illegible copy or missing punctuation.
All classified ads will appear on the web at www.carpenocturne.net/classifieds.
Attach your completed ad to an e-mail as a file in either of the above formats and send to:
Ads@CarpeNocturne.net.
If you want your ad to be "clickable," please state that in your e-mail and give the link
you'd like it directed to.

For any questions, please feel free to contact Ads@CarpeNocturne.net.

All advertisers receive one copy of Carpe Nocturne Magazine per paid ad.

beats antique

By Kathleen Sharkey

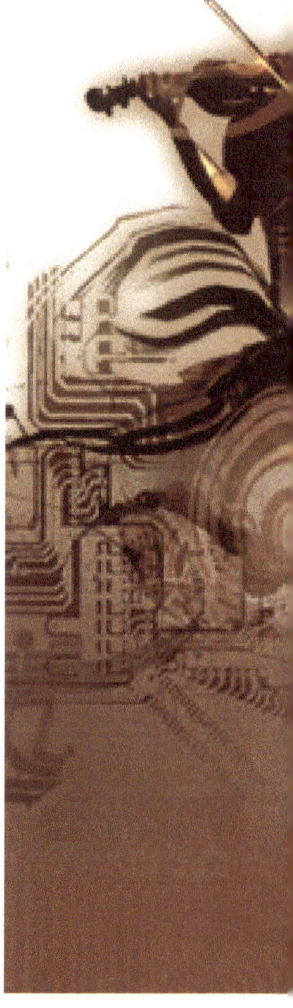

Each tempo hit is a muscle drop, each bowstring draw is a fluid motion. Visualization of music in the beauty of an amazing dancer, her every move a graceful representation. No real lyrics just flowing music from violin, saz, drums and whatever else happens to be available. Fusion they call it, fusing cultural music iconography into modern experimental music. I call it a traveling museum of beauty and sound.

David Satori, a jack-of-all-trades musician, is originally from Vermont. His love of music from an early age brought him to the California Institute of the Arts where he received degrees in music, performance and composition. While in California Satori started The Funnies, releasing two albums during their time together. 2003 brought him to the band Aphrodesia with whom he traveled to Nigeria, West Africa and Lagos where Satori produced their 2007 album Lagos by Bus.

Upon his return to San Francisco he started dating the remarkable and stunning Zoe Jakes a lifelong dancer; jazz, ballet, tango, Indian and her love, Belly Dancing. Zoe had traveled with Yard Dogs Road Show, worked with the Extra Marching band, where she met drummer Tommy Cappel, and toured with The Indigo Belly Dance Company. She began working with Miles Copeland in 2005 while touring with Belly dance Superstars.

Tommy Cappel, another World Music fan, is from Virginia and has also been playing music from childhood. With a studio drumming degree from Berklee College of Music Cappel was the perfect addition to what was slowly becoming what is now Beats Antique.

So in 2007 these three fabulously talented people formed Beats Antique in San Francisco. They had already worked together for a Burning Man decompression party and they knew each other well. So they decided to create music that would harmonize with Zoe's amazing dance ability. With the help of Miles Copeland they released their first album Tribal Derivations. Zoe became the dancer/producer/arranger with David on varied instruments and Tommy on drums. Their second album Collide was more than well received placing in the top ten of the most downloaded World Music albums. Even more musical instruments, in the form of collaborative friends joined the band for their third album Contraptions Vol. 1. Every album after kept the variety going, always finding a new way to present their musical concepts in every new incarnation. Contraptions Vol. 1 was followed in 2010 by The Trunk Archives EP and Blind Threshold, then, in 2011 Elektrafone, 2012 Contraption Vol. 2, 2013 A Thousand Faces Act I and most recently in 2014 A Thousand Faces Act II.

It is really hard to describe Beats Antique in words. Their performances are like musical synesthesia with Zoe representing the visual representation of the music, and synesthesia is a very personal concept. There are definitely Asian and Indian influences in the music (I call these different influences though I do know that India is in Asia). Blended in with Turkish, hip-hop, afro-beat and electronic, as well as any other type of instrument they can fuse in, that is Beats Antique. They have an amazing presence on youtube, https://www.youtube.com/channel/UCTuoFZbyKJzm1YHycQXg2EA, and really the only way to understand the magnitude of amazing that is Beats Antique is to see them perform. Their newest tour Creature Carnival will start October 15 in Madison, WI and will run through November 8. Full tour information can be found here: http://www.creaturecarnival.net/. If you can go see them live it will be an experience never to forget.

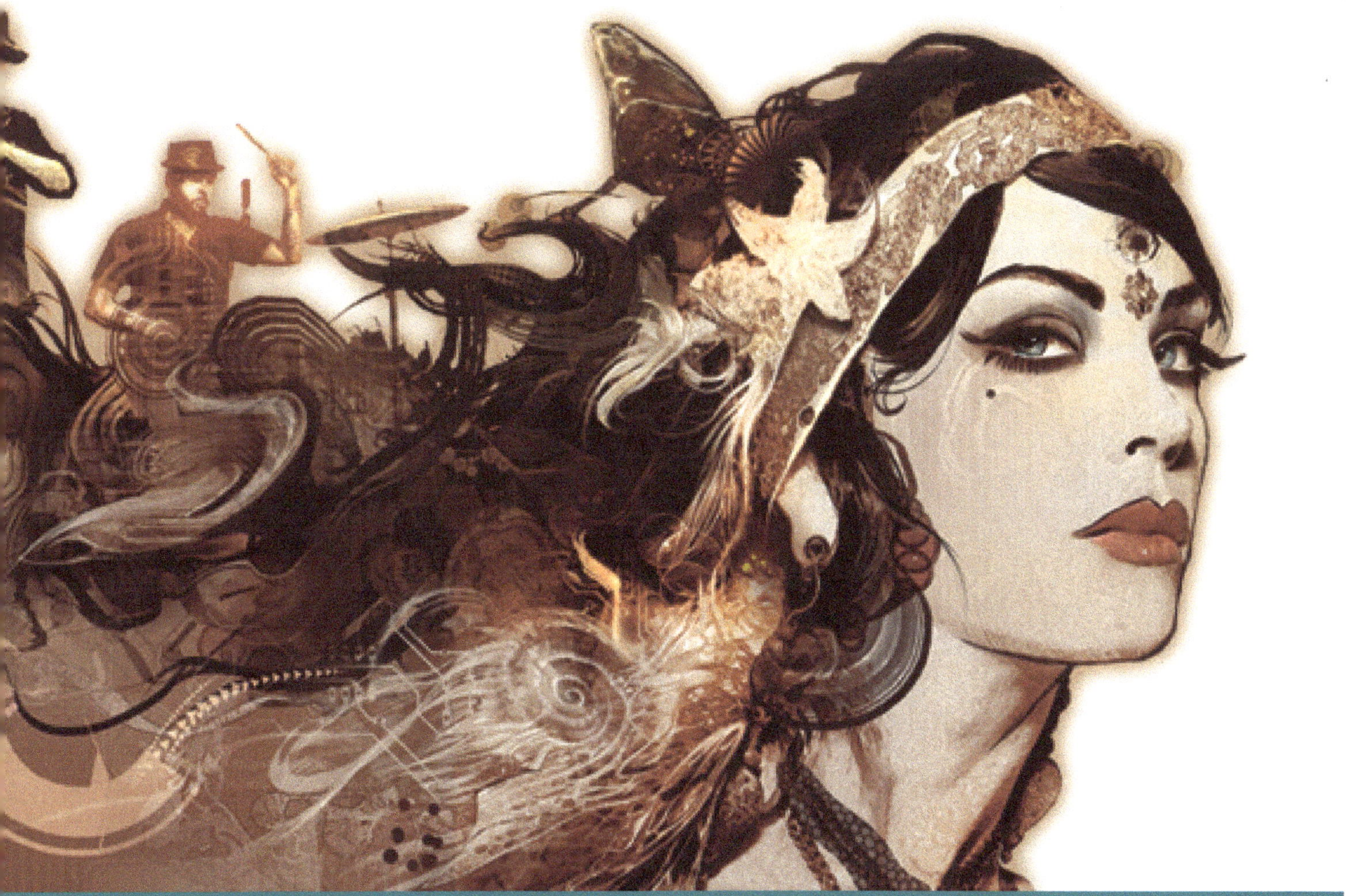

> *Their performances are like musical synesthesia... and synesthesia is a very personal concept."*

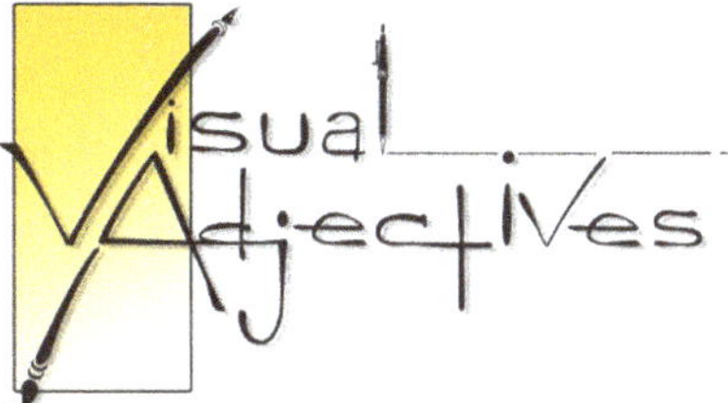

Ad agencies and graphic designers charge anywhere from $500 to $5,000 to design and layout print quality, hi-res ads. Carpe Nocturne Magazine's in-house design staff can help you build the perfect ad for your company. With client supplied hi-res images and copy, prices range from $35 to $150 depending on size and client specifications.

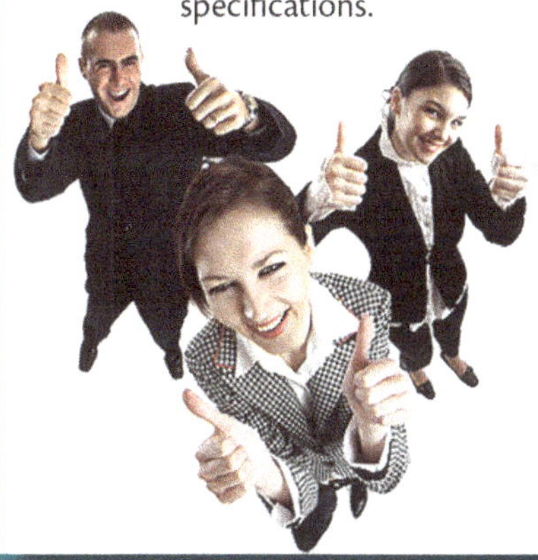

DARK SHIMMIES

Westminster, MD

October 11-12th

Sponsored by Yasaman Vrd'dhi

www.DarkShimmies.com

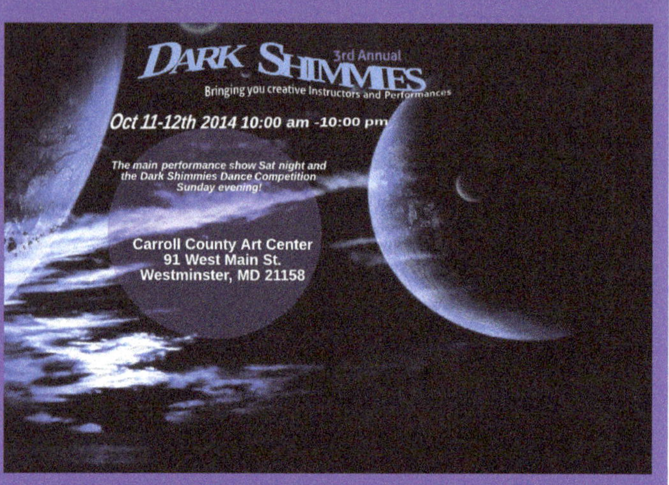

WAKING PERSEPHONE

Seattle, WA

October 17-19th

Sponsored by Tempest

www.wakingpersephone.com

OOKY SPOOKY

Kalamazoo, MI

October 25-26th

Sponsored by Boheme Tribal

www.bohemetribal.com

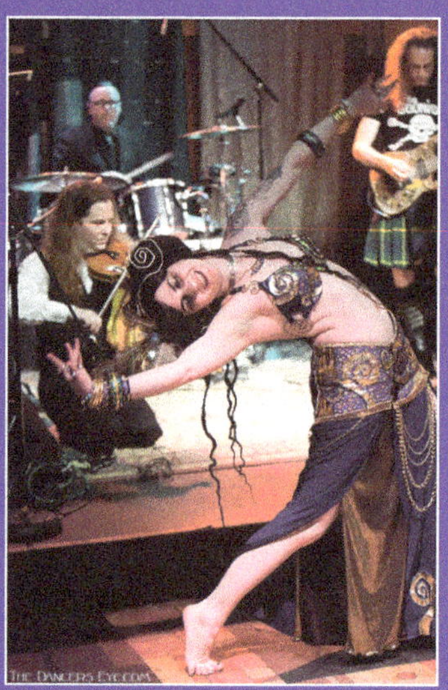

1001 NIGHTS,

featuring Mira Betz

Lexington, KY

November 21-23rd

Sponsored by Mecca Live Studio & Gallery

www.MeccaDance.com

3RD COAST TRIBAL

Ft. Worth, TX

January 8-11, 2015

Featuring Ariellah, Zoe Jakes, Donna Mejia,

Tamalyn Dallal & more!

http://3rdcoasttribal.us/index.html

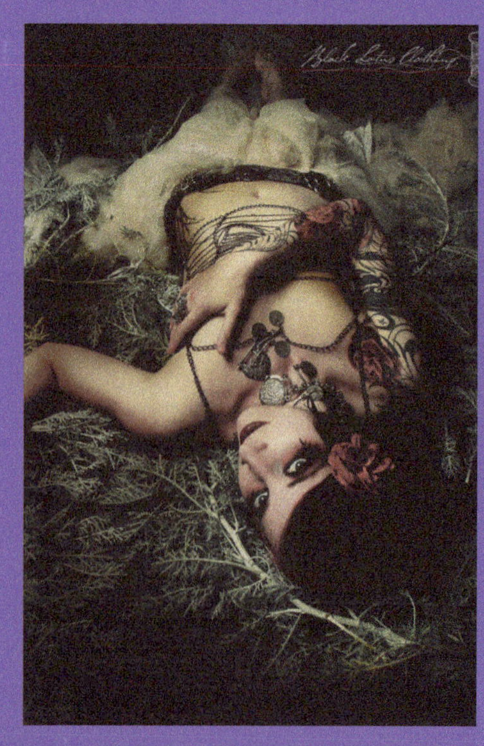

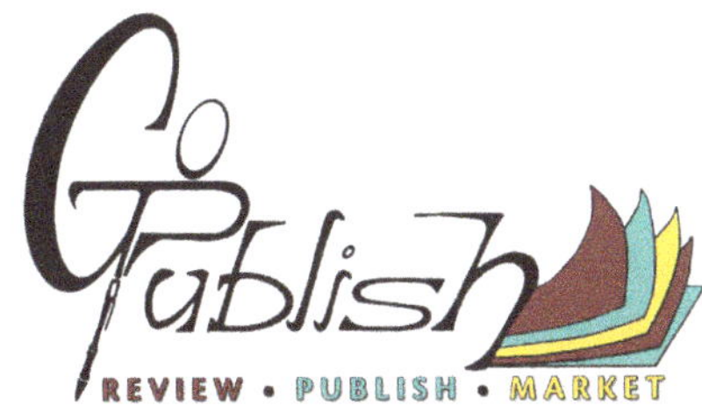

PUBLISHING PACKAGES
MARKETING PACKAGES
EDITORIAL SERVICES
REVIEW PACKAGES

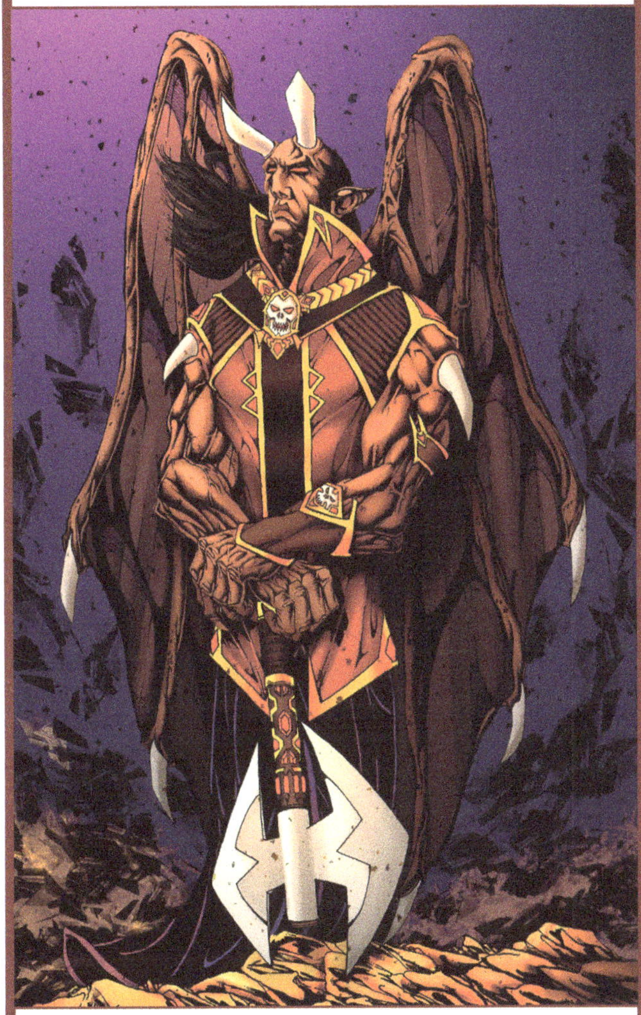

TRANSFORM YOUR STORY INTO A BOOK
SO GOPUBLISHYOURBOOK.COM

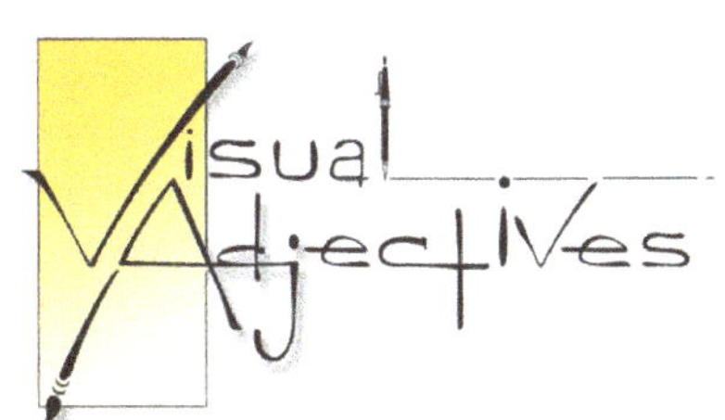

COMMISSION ARTWORK FOR
YOUR PROJECT OR NOVEL!

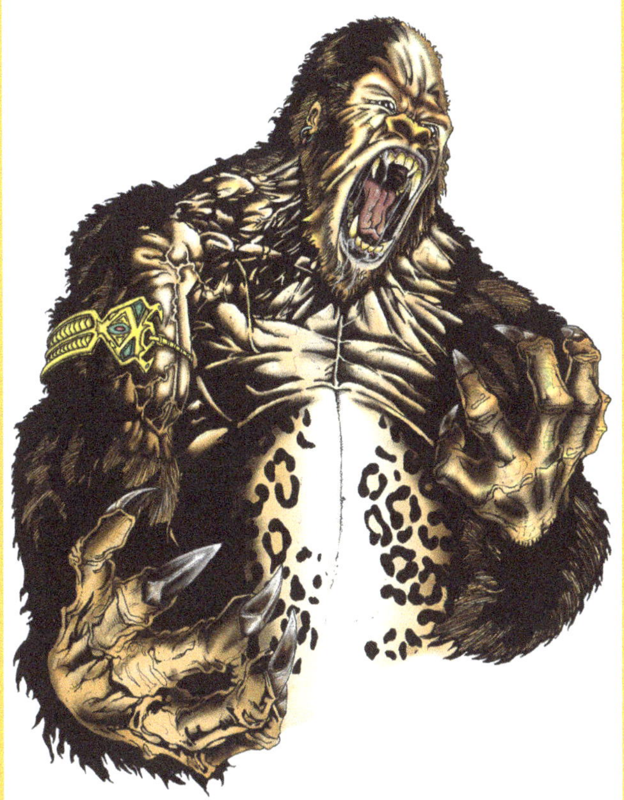

PRODUCTION SERVICES
Comic Book • Graphic Novels • Illustrated Novels

CONCEPT SERVICE
Writer • Sketches • Storyboard
ILLUSTRATION SERVICE
Illustrator • Colorist
FULL SERVICE
Writer • Sketches • Storyboard • Illustrator
Colorist • Letterer • Cover • Editor
INDIVIDUAL SERVICE
Writer • Sketches • Storyboard • Penciler • Inker
Illustrator • Colorist • Letterer • Cover • Editor

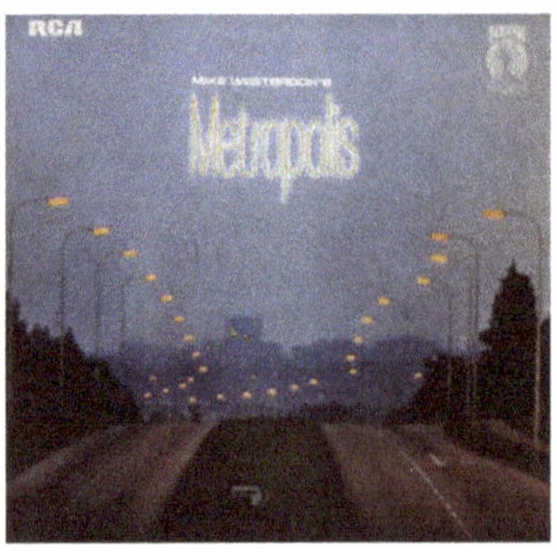

MIKE WESTBROOK
"METROPOLIS"
Label: RCA
1971

Like a mirage at the end of the empty road, in the impending evening, the shadow of a city appears on the background, beyond the street lights. Mike Westbrook's Metropolis is not only a well-known (at least among British jazz lovers) suite in nine movements, but something like a feverish fragment of life.

Jazz improvisations, avant-garde and some rock splinters that reflect the spirit and style of the period in which the music was composed, until the final theme - 'Part IX' - played by Harry Beckett, that closes this work in an incredibly evocative way. His trumpet is lyrical and introspective, the perfect translation in sounds of a possible noir story.

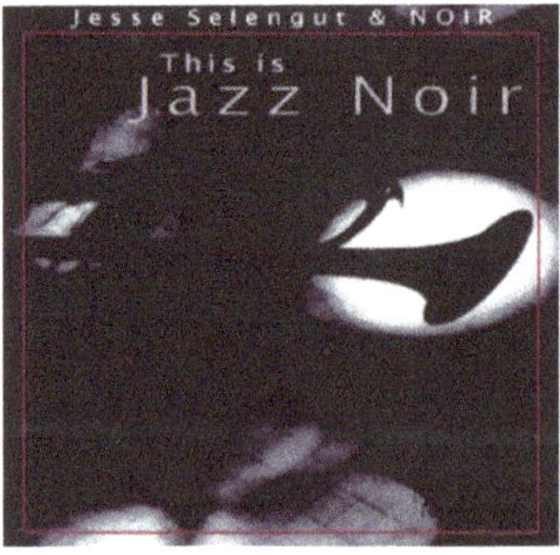

JESSE SELENGUT & NOIR
"THIS IS JAZZ NOIR"
Label: Jesse Selengut & Noir
2006

'Key Laser' opens this album in pure (Miles Davis) film noir trumpet sound, first step into a fizzy fusion of deep, thoughtful jazz and nervous electro grooves, spiced with some latin flavour. Jesse Selengut & NOIR are a formidable rhythm machine, fascinated by dark boulevards, dirty puddles and tempting nocturnal lights. A world in black'n'white with just some burst of sun.

"We are in the neighborhood of Darkwave City of course, and some songs are absolutey ready for the art of David Lynch or Christopher Nolan."

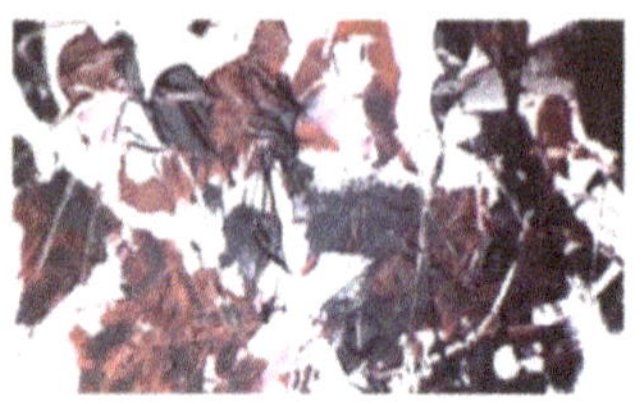

SHUTEYES
"BEATS AND ALPHABETICS"
Label: Dopecrates
2010

Here is something worthy of the most renowned rap artists. Beat and Alphabetics is an amazing, small magic box which produces sounds and filters ideas for the right side of the brain. It is surprising how this young musician easily and sapiently handles a certain hip hop lexicon so strongly influencend by jazz.

'Noir Jazz Spots', in particular, also thanks to its awesome intro, is a piece that lives in a perfect balance between rhythm, sampling and words, able to create a dramatic, estrange atmosphere. No doubt, this guy is a whizz.

CHAINED SHADOWS

A Gathering of Things in Noir Style.

by SERGIO MANGHINA

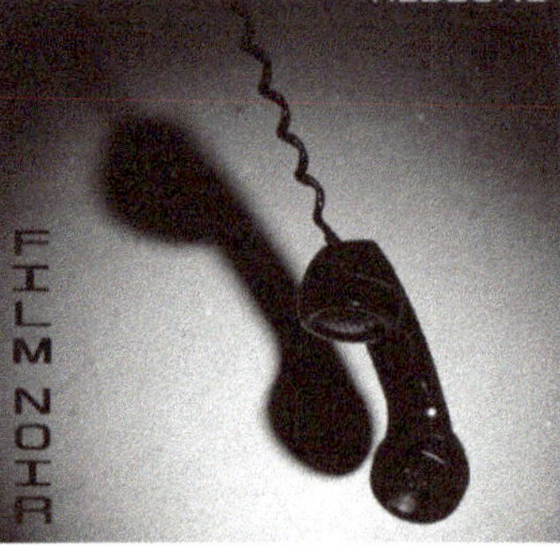

REDZONE
"FILM NOIR" single
Label: Phasechange
2010

Since 1997, the London based Redzone - Amy, Justin and Tim - are appreciated for their capacity as experimenters in producing sounds and use of new media. At first sight, their sinister trip hop could remember of Portishead, but they are definitely more cold and bristly than the Bristolians.

'Film Noir' is crossed by electronic shudders, an unquiet

drum'n'bass just mitigated by the ethereal voice of Amy. These guys are very skilled in recording with their own samples, creating seductive moods. Great cover art - photo by Many Ayromlou - conceptually evocative.

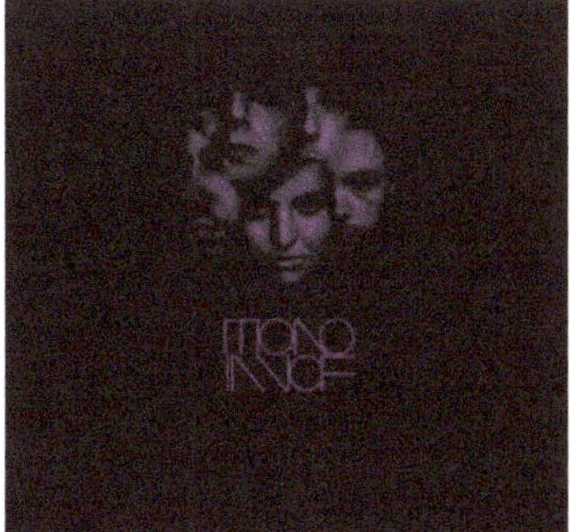

MONO IN VCF
"MONO IN VCF"
Label: Stylo Music
2008

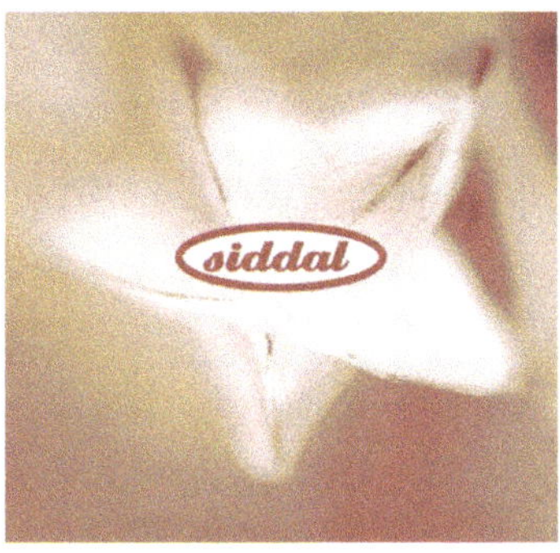

SIDDAL
"MYSTERY AND THE SEA" EP
Label: Bedazzled
1997

Caution with these two bands! Their massive dose of dream pop, shoegaze and slowcore, filtered by haunting female voices, and hypnotic guitars, could be unhealthy for you. We are in the neighborhood of Darkwave City, of course, and some songs are absolutely ready for the art of David Lynch or Christopher Nolan.

For example, songs like 'Spider Rotation' by Mono In VCF and 'Just Around The Corner' by Siddal are pure ethereal -noir innervated by unquiet and perturbed moods.

There is always something or someone behind the corner. Maybe it's just a shadow. Maybe..

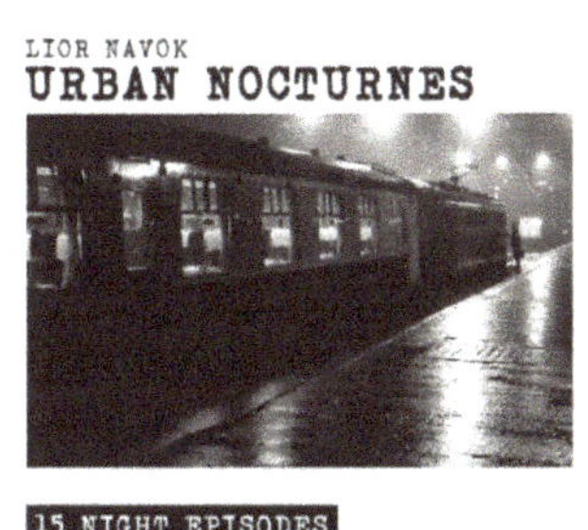

LIOR NAVOK
"URBAN NOCTURNES!"
Label: NLM
2011

Lior Navok is an Israeli composer of rare sensitivity. These nightly soundscapes for solo piano appear slowly on the surface like images after a nitrate bath in the dark-room. It is classical contemporary music with some inevitable

roughness but also a strong jazz flavour. So, everyone will find his own right piece of emotion among these haunting shadows.

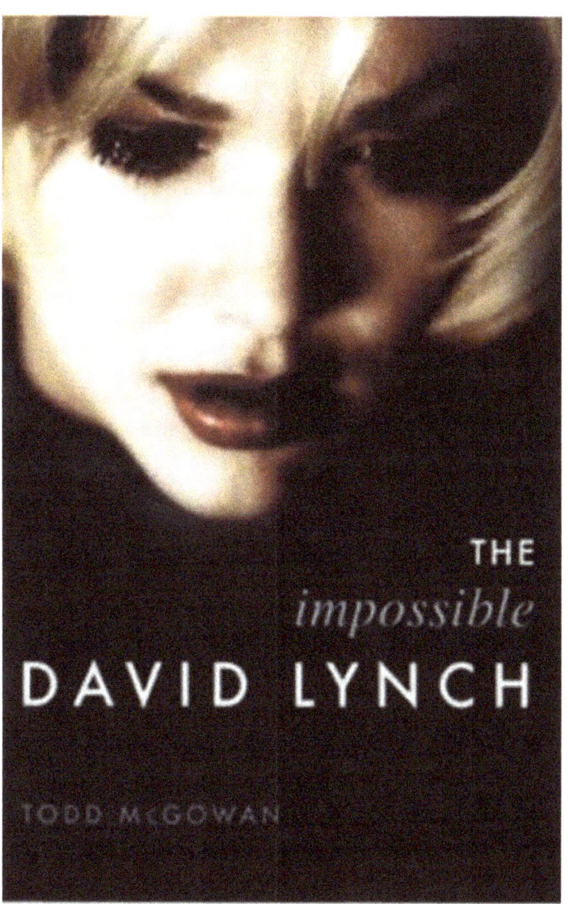

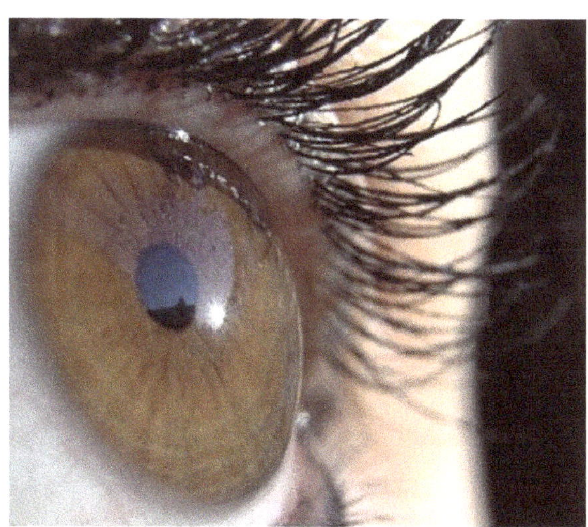

FILM DIRECTION, PERFECTED:
PROFILE OF CHRISTOPHER
NOLAN

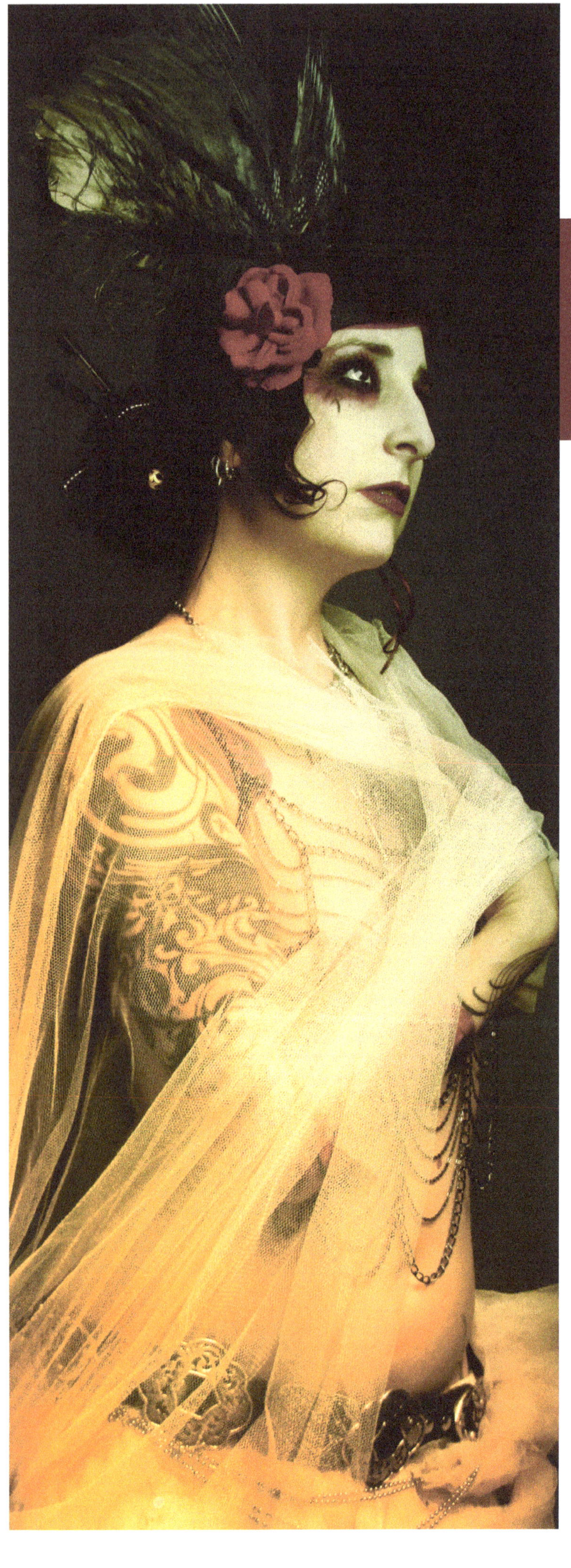

DANCES IN T

I t's nearly impossible to have a conversation about Gothic or Dark Fusion Belly Dance and not discuss the influence of Ariellah. Based in San Francisco, Ariellah began her belly dancing career in 2001, studying with Janine Ryle (of Danse Mahgreb) and Rachel Brice. Her previous twelve-year classical ballet training with the Royal Academy of Dance in London provided her with a solid foundation of discipline, daily practice, and flawless technique. She teaches her unique style of modern belly dance all over the world. During one of her few breaks from touring, she took the time to discuss her annual dark arts showcase "ShadowDance" and to share some advice on belly dancing.

Carpe Nocturne: What was your inspiration for "Shadow Dance"?

Ariellah: In order to speak about my inspiration for ShadowDance, I must first speak about how it began...

(The following exerpt was written by DJ Amar:)

"IN THE BEGINNING...

It started with a blue haired girl from DC, a DJ, a drummer and a couple of the bay area's proponents of the Gothic Belly Dance scene.

In the summer of '06, shortly after meeting Mavi at a Tribal Belly Dance festival, Amar saw a post on tribe and received an email from said blue haired girl about coming to California that November and wondering if there were any shows around that time that she could go to. Both Amar and Tempest replied and began discussing putting together a 'little' show in Oakland. Amar emailed a rather large group of dancers, figuring maybe 20-30% would be available and 2007 added workshops and vendors to the mix. 2008 kicked it up another notch with a spectacular new venue, 2 rooms, theater shows and sideshows, midnight gallery,

HE SHADOWS...
...EVER DARKER

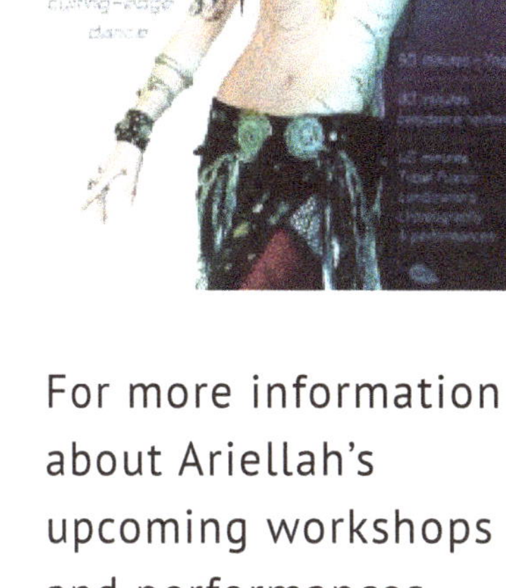

say yes. Oops! It turned out Every Single dancer he contacted said yes, and we had a potential show that was too big for the original little dive bar show we had in mind.

Later that summer, on a trip to Portland, Amar and Ariellah met at a dark fusion belly dance show that they were both performing at. Shortly after returning, Tempest mentioned bringing Ariellah in to put on the show together. How could That be a bad idea? Ariellah graciously agreed. We added Sooozhyq to the production team and began planning the show, booked the Oakland Metro and came up with the title "Shadowdance".

The first Show was a sold out success and an amazing night. We decided to do another the following year, which was just as amazing with completely new performances that were out of this world.

fire, an elixer bar and more. Ariellah and Amar produced Shadowdance 2008 together at Orbis Nex.

After 3 years of pouring their hearts into these spectacular shows, Ariellah and Amar's schedules called for a break to focus on touring and other creative projects, as well as Ariellah's marriage to Bruce.

In 2010, Ariellah takes the reigns and brings back ShadowDance bigger and DARKER than ever."

Ariellah: Since I took over sole production of ShadowDance, I have truly focused on bringing the underground "dark" artists of all kinds, to the surface. These artists have allowed me to present their talents to a broader public audience and bring the dark arts to light, so to speak...

For more information about Ariellah's upcoming workshops and performances, visit www.ariellah.com and www.deshretdance.com.

...I wanted to create a dark world that all could enjoy and find beauty and solace."

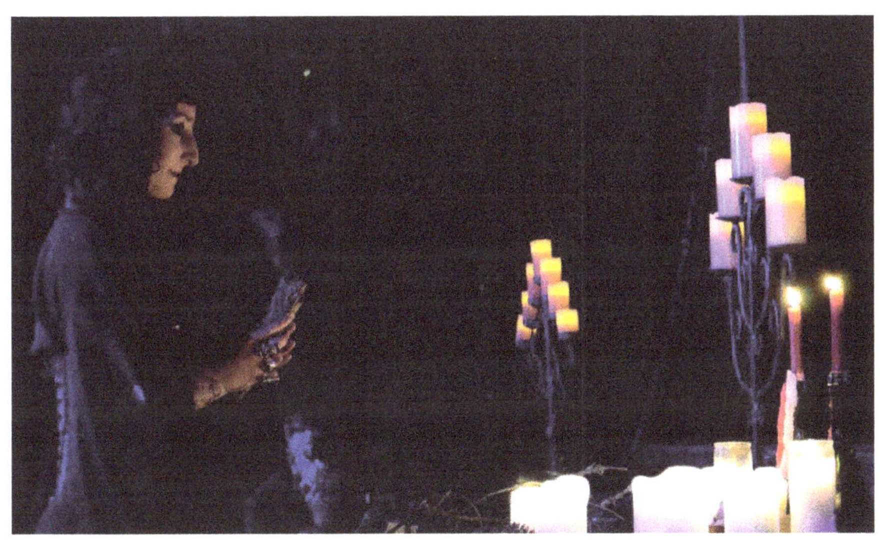

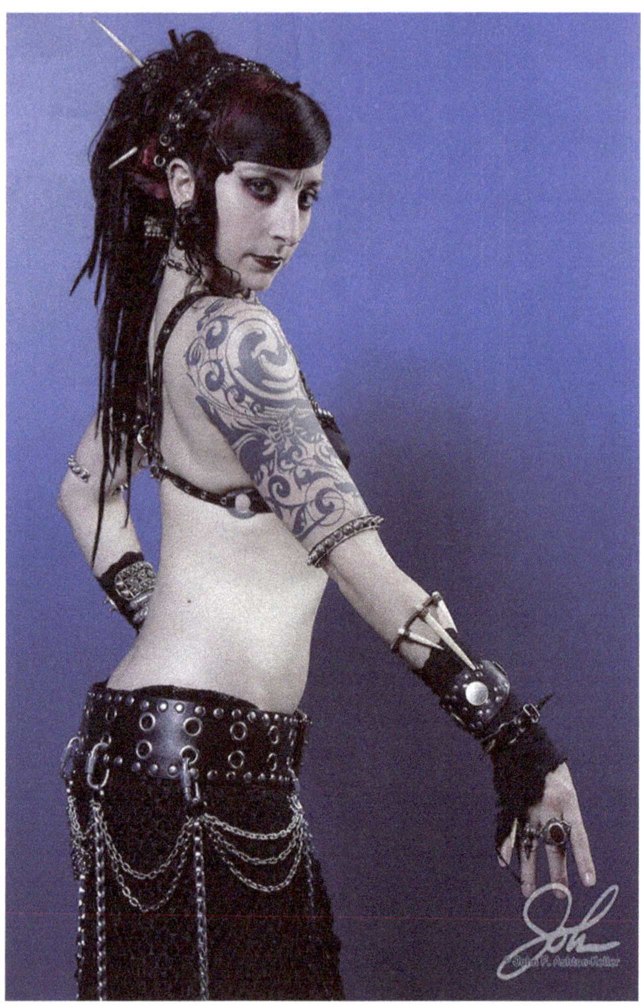

My inspiration comes from the artists whom I come into contact with, year after year. My inspiration comes from my own life experience and how I have found such beauty and depth in "darkness". ShadowDance allows each artist to portray their own perceptions, ideas, notions, feelings and thoughts on this vast subject matter... the subject matter of darkness. However the artist wants to interpret that word/concept/idea/subject, is what comes to life on the ShadowDance stage.

CN: Why did you decide to direct your own show?

A: I believe it to be a purely selfish endeavor, in that I wanted to attend a show where the "darker" side of life, the depth of it all, the full range of human emotions, and nature was beautifully portrayed. There are performers whom I admire all over the world, and I want to include their talents in my show and present them to the public. These artists might not ever have this particular kind of opportunity, OR these particular artists may not usually present their art publicly, and so I am lucky enough to be able to have them on my stage.

I also hoped to create a space where the audience FEELS something when they attend this event... from the moment they walk into the theatre, to the moment they set foot out of the door. They come into a world that most may not have the privilege of seeing... it is like walking into my private home...or the private crevices of my mind; what I find beautiful, pleasing, deep, passionate, artistic, and dark.

My intention is also to allow music to be a major factor at this event... musical selections are painstakingly selected and presented from the moment the guests arrive as they walk in the door, to create a certain dark and emotional ambiance, mood and atmosphere. We have guest gothic DJs every year and they play at the intermissions and also after the theatre show is over. Chairs are immediately removed and the black box theatre becomes a gothic night club where everyone is invited to stay and dance to their hearts content or simply take in the dark sounds. ShadowDance always has 2-4 live musical acts as well... to give homage to the beauty that is music, the muse that is music. The impetus for all things...

So in a nutshell, I wanted to create a dark world that all could enjoy and find beauty and solace. And we have had incredible feedback from the least removed guests who are not at all immersed in the gothic subculture who come back every year or are brand new and have told me how deeply they enjoy this event! It has been a great joy to see this "wall" so to speak, being brought down and I enjoy hearing and seeing the reactions to this event from people of all cultures, walks of life, performance artists and non artists, goths and non goths, dancers and non dancers and the list goes on and on.

CN: How has the show grown over the years?

A: It started off very strong, fortunately, with incredible artists gracing the stage from the very first year, as DJ Amar mentioned in the passage above, and from this, we have built such a loyal guest base, who return year after year. We have been fortunate to be able to maintain this high level of performance art throughout the years, and have built up quite an incredible reputation of being a beautiful, wonderful, and powerful show, and a well run show at that! We have had sold out shows almost every year for the past 4 years! It has grown so much in reputation that I have artists asking ME if they can be in the show! It has been a great joy to see this event grow into such a beautiful creature.

CN: How many weekends do you spend traveling and what is one of your favorite places to visit?

A: I would say, on average, I am gone 2 weekends a month, and some months it could be more. My very favourite places to visit are Italy, Germany and Buenos Aires, Mexico City, and Rio de Janeiro... the reasons for this are numerous!!

CN: What is your favorite part of being on the seminar circuit?

A: Most definitely my favourite part of teaching workshops is THE

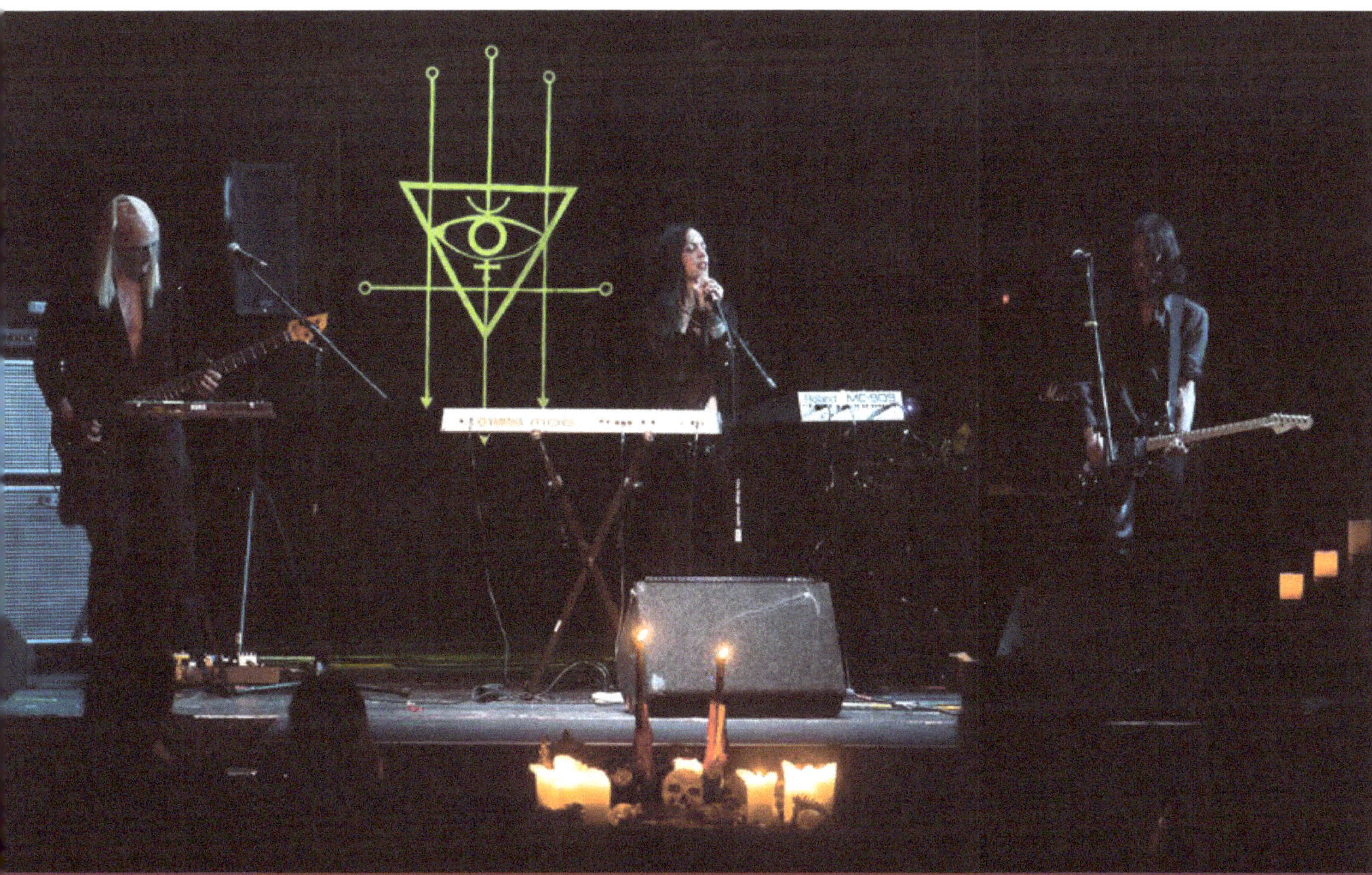

DANCERS! It is a great joy for me to work with the dancers of the world on bettering and respecting our art form and not only that, but I have made some of the most wonderful connections and have found a loving family in my dance sisters and brothers and for that I am ever grateful. I love working with both new and old students, and I especially love seeing the progression of many of my long-time students and how they become strong dancers in their own right... it makes my heart smile and sing!

CN: How are the belly dance communities different in other parts of the world?

A: I actually believe that most of our dance communities are very similar in a way... they all have their growing pains, growth spurts, new generations and old generations. I think you find more motivated countries and some spoiled countries, some fast growing countries and some newer to this art form and all of them are wonderful in their own way!

CN: Your suggestion to read "The Creative Habit" by Twyla Tharp is something I still share with my students. Are there any other books or websites you can recommend to belly dancers?

A: "The Creative Habit" offers a wealth of knowledge and great exercises to get the dancer to understand better the creative processes, and I think its one of the best "dance" books out there. I have an extensive list of dance books and rather than list them here, I would invite dancers to email me at: info@ariellah.com, mention this interview and I shall send them the reading list. I would also encourage dancers to partake of my yearly weeklong intensive programs or my 3-day intensive immersion program, as they are required to read off my reading list as homework prior to the intensives and during the intensive. I do hand out my complete reading list, as a resource for the dancer after they leave my intensive program.

Just for a teaser, I will list my top three other favourite reference books: (these are books I look to over and over again)

"Psychology of Dance" by Ceci Taylor and Jim Taylor

- enhances your capabilities of understanding your strengths and weaknesses and gives you mental tools to enhance your dance practice

"Intimate Act of Choreography" by Lynne Anne Blom and L. Tarin Chaplin

- gives the dancer a plethora of exercises that will help make more dynamic choreographies and also discusses structure, form, movement and intention

"The Art of Making Dances" by Doris Humphrey

- incredible source book for choreography

CN: If you could go back in time and give yourself three pieces of advice when you first began performing belly dance, what would those be?

A: I was VERY lucky in that my dance path had a natural and strong evolution to it. Nothing was forced, there was no goal or ulterior motive, and I happened to be in the right places at the right times and ended up studying with one of the most incredible belly dancers of our time and possibly even in history, and I attribute much of my seamless belly dance journey to her incredible teachings. I somehow naturally heeded the following advice, but this is advice that I would give to all beginning belly dancers:

1.   Belly dance is a very complex, intricate and difficult art form... try not to get discouraged easily. Stay dedicated and focused and know that you WILL be able to master the movements. Consistent practice is the key. Even when it feels like your body will never get a particular movement, know that it will, I 100% guarantee it, with practice. You can do anything and reach any goal that you desire, you just need to put in the effort... your body will get it, I promise!

2.   Do not be in a rush! I cannot stress this enough... the only way to know this dance form intricately is to practice diligently. The only way you can master something is through practice, and the only way to become a good performing artist is through your practice and through many, many years of performing experience. There is no fast track to becoming a good dancer or teacher. It all comes with time. And I believe, to truly respect our art form, you must fully understand good and proper technique and also the history of the dance... and you must have an intimate physical understanding of each movement and also a knowledge of how to "dance safely" without injury. Without this knowledge, experience, and first hand understanding, in my opinion, you disrespect this beautiful art form. Please know that you WILL become a beautiful, strong dancer and teacher, but that it takes time. Allow yourself the time to immerse yourself in this dance form and the time to cultivate strong technique and also your own personal artistic dance style and understanding of performance art and all of its many aspects. You will become such a gift to future generations of this dance form and will have left a legitimate and respectful legacy in your wake.

3.   Be yourself, be unique, be creative, don't be afraid to be vulnerable. You are a human being, you are an artist, you are a dancer and you have something to say. We want to hear your story, we want to see the way that you express yourself and your view of life and emotion and all that is in between. Try not to be afraid to make yourself vulnerable and try not to be afraid to dance with your own voice. Be humble in your offerings. Give your art to the world; let it be for yourself but also, give it away and let it be for the community. Be sure to have strong technique to back up your creativity and to have the tools you need in order to have the freedom to fully express yourself. Do not forget that you are a unique person and that we are all listening to what you have to say about our world... your world... take us into your world... the more authentic and honest you can be, the more we will be captivated, interested and understanding about your art.

CN: What new projects are you working on?

A: I am currently working with Frederique (www.LadyFred.com) on our new Silent Sirens Theatre "play". I am also currently working on creating my 2nd instructional DVD! And... I am working on bringing a theatre show to the stage in the bay area in 2015 that takes a very different and unique approach to dance theatre, and I hope to be able to speak more about this as this project comes to fruition, but know that this idea has been in my head and on my to do list for about 5 years now, and I think it is about time to bring it to life!

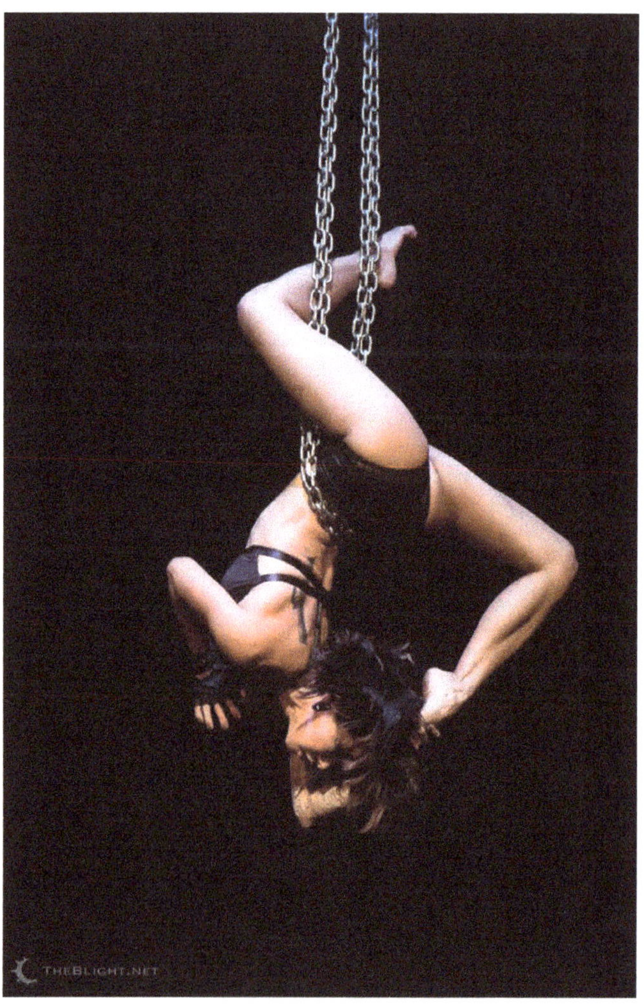

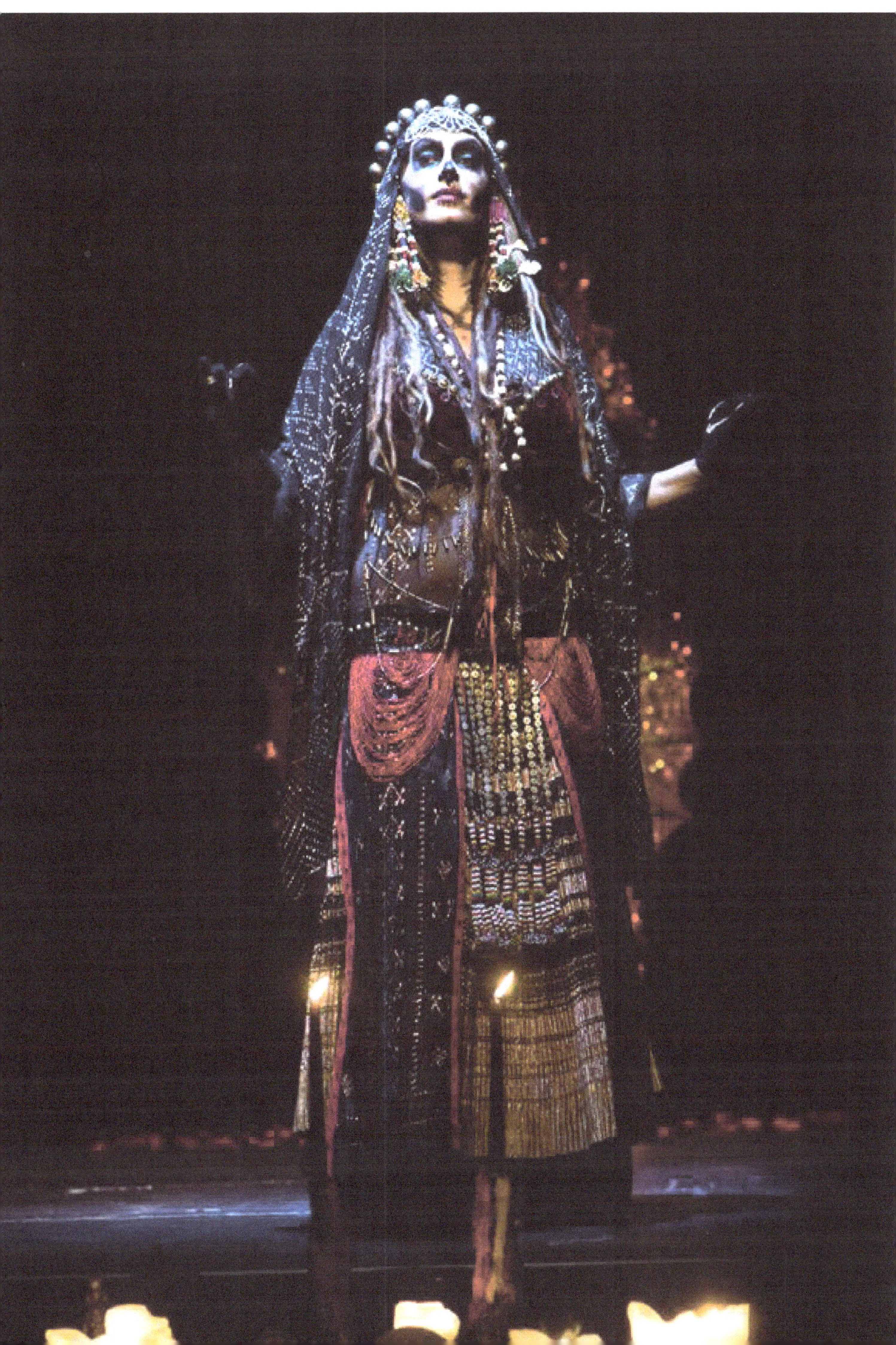

DIY BLUSH & BRONZER

By Isolde de Mortimer

There are loads of reasons to try DIY makeup. Maybe you want to save money or avoid potentially harmful chemicals that may be present in mass manufactured products. Perhaps you have sensitive skin or don't want to use products that are tested on animals or maybe you're just the crafty type who likes to create and wants to customize an exact color for yourself. Whatever the reason, do-it-yourself blushes and bronzers are easy to make.

INGREDIENTS

Arrowroot powder or cornstarch*
Hibiscus powder (red)
Beetroot powder (pink)
Cocoa power (brown)
Cinnamon (golden)
Teaspoon
Container
Lavender essential oil (optional, and not for sensitive skin)

*Arrowroot powder is available at health food stores or online. Cornstarch is likely in your pantry, but if your goal is to avoid potentially harmful ingredients like GMO's, you'll want to use organic.

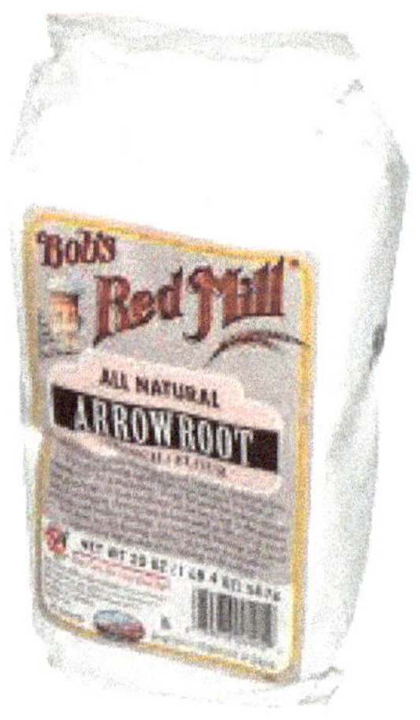

DIRECTIONS

For blush:

Beetroot

Start with one teaspoon of your base, either arrowroot or cornstarch in your container. Add two teaspoons of either hibiscus or beetroot powder depending if you want your blush more red or pink, and mix it up. Test the color on your skin. Like it? Want more red? More pink? Use additional hibiscus or beetroot. Add a little at a time because while you can add more of your base powder to lighten the color, you'll be creating more and more blush. Test again. Want more depth? You may wish to try adding a touch of cocoa or cinnamon. Experiment conservatively until you have just the color you like. If you like fragrance, you can tap in a drop of lavender essential oil and mix thoroughly. A word of caution: lavender essential oil is safe for topical use, but it can be sensitizing for some skin so if you're the sensitive type, it's best to leave out the lavender oil.

Hibiscus

For bronzer:

Use one teaspoon of your base powder of choice and add one teaspoon of cocoa and one teaspoon of cinnamon. Mix well in your container,

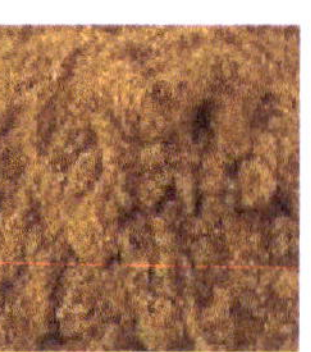

Cinnamon

breaking up any clumps. Apply to your skin to check the color. Add a little more brown or golden color depending on your liking, proceeding cautiously so as not to get too dark. Adding a pinch of pink beetroot can be flattering too.

Make notes as you create so you'll remember what worked and what didn't. Once you have that perfect shade, you can duplicate it later.

Make small batches of your blush and bronzer since it won't have any preservatives. If after a while you notice any changes to the smell, appearance, or texture of your DIY makeup, throw it out and make more.

If you're not used to using loose blush or bronzer, it's a little different than pressed makeup. Dip your brush in, tap off the excess, and apply. Repeat those steps, blending the edges, until you reach

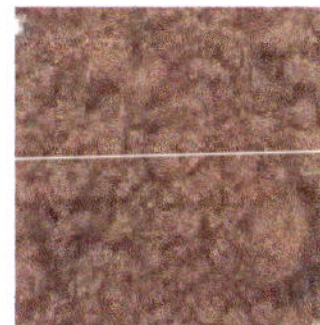

Cocoa

the desired coverage and color depth. Tapping the brush before application is important as excess powder will fall onto other areas of your face if you don't shake it off first. You'll get the hang of it after some practice.

While the formula isn't as elegant as commercially produced cosmetics, it still works and is fun to make. Invite friends and have a blush making bash! Custom bronzer is also a unique gift. Blend it up, package it in a cute container and you have a one-of-a-kind present. Just experiment and have fun!

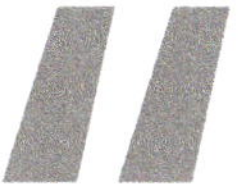

Make notes as you create so you'll remember what worked and what didn't."

SUBSCRIBE

Carpe Nocturne Magazine is a quarterly publication available worldwide. In addition, we publish a digital magazine that is a duplicate of the print edition, advertisements and all. When you advertise in the print edition of Carpe Nocturne Magazine, your ad automatically appears in the digital magazine. Our paid subscribers have the magazine delivered to their home or office.

DIGITAL EDITION
Never miss an Issue!
Receive your digital magazine in an instant. Enjoy your favorite magazine on your Tablet, Phone, or Desktop. Page after page of exclusive interview, reports and current news delivered direct to your desktop or mobile device quarterly.

The digital edition is exactly the same as a print edition but with additional powerful interactive features to enhance your reading experience.

Carpe Nocturne Magazine offers you exclusive content with high quality photos and the ability to view videos and click links straight from the magazine page.

With your FREE digital subscription, Carpe Nocturne Magazine will show up in your inbox as soon as the new issue is published.

PRINT EDITION
Don't miss an issue. Have Carpe Nocturne Magazine delivered to your home or office. Purchase a subscription for yourself or someone you know, and Carpe Nocturne Magazine will land in your mailbox 4 times a year.

Carpe Nocturne Magazine
ATTN: Subscribe
14280 Military Trail, #7501
Delray Beach, FL 33482

Please be sure to include the mailing address where you want your subscription to be sent.

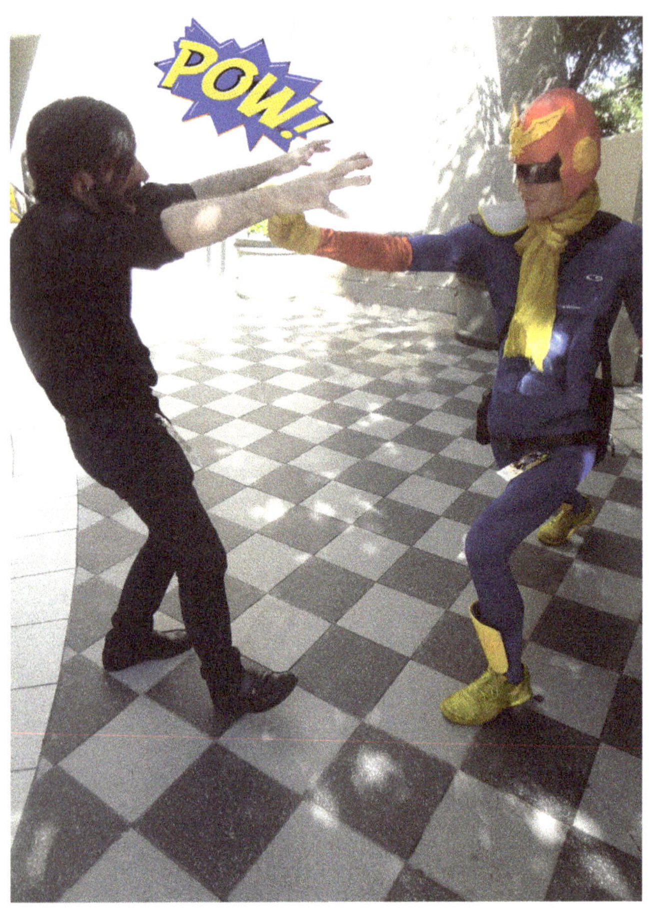

Surviving Homeland Security, Atlanta traffic and about a thousand Alabama football fans, we finally arrived at the Omni Hotel by the CNN center to begin three days of the most awesome geekdom one could hope to experience. One by one the roomies arrived and armed with lightsabers, props, costumes (or lack thereof for the ladies) and over $400 of liquor we made our way into the humid sultry southern night. And into the arms of what may best be called Tribe. Thousands upon thousands of like-minded Sci-Fi, Horror, Gamer, Science, RPG and Fantasy fans. DragonCon had begun!

In 2013 there were more than 62,000 people dressed to impress streaming through the halls and streets of downtown Atlanta. And I have met and made friends with folk from as far as Eastern Europe and Australia. All who come for the event and the revelry. Fans of every genre imaginable spend the whole year scrutinizing and creating cosplays that are screen accurate to the type of materials or buttons used in the movie or TV show from which their love came. Others re-imagine or recreate new versions or imaginings of their favorite characters, bending genre, creed, race and gender to pay homage to their heroes and villains. The result is nothing less than spectacular. Add to the mix over 400 celebrities, artists, musicians, scientists, authors and profession-

als (and more than a few sips of the traditional "pie") and you have three days of geek bliss.

For the uninitiated and soon to be first time attendee con virgins, I would like to share some facts and advice.

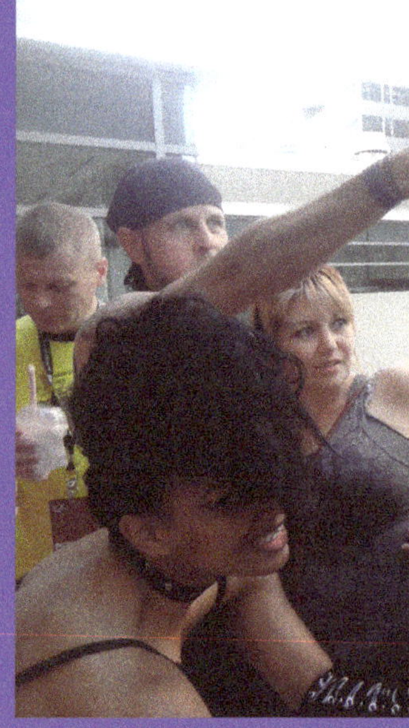

First, before you even get to con, remember to start your costumes and cosplays early! Facebook is swamped with Memes regarding the tedious but enjoyable task of creating your look. And with good reason. Life does not wait. Life never does. And if you think you can put together a screen accurate Iron Man, Sith Lord or Sailor Moon two weeks before flying out, all I can do is wish you the best! I know this from experience. I helped my best friend put together her Akasha from Queen of the Damned and we started it a month early. The night before we flew out, involved three Monsters and a 5 Hour Energy Shot. We were literally hot glue gunning two hours before the flight! Don't wait! Start now!

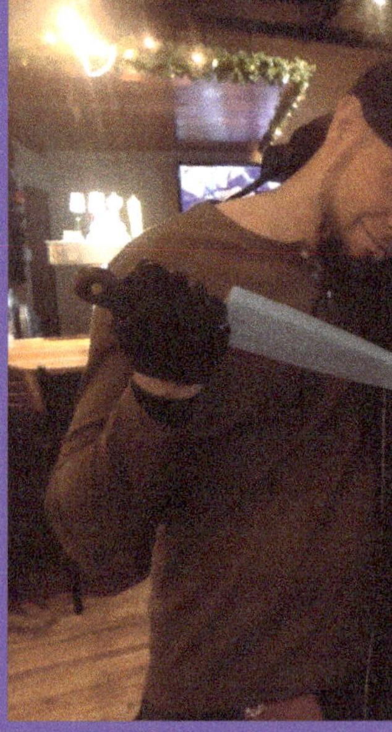

Getting there is a challenge all its own. First, if you are flying remember that TSA does not smile kindly upon weapons. If you think you can get through security with Mal's sidearm or your favorite Mjolnir at your side, you are in for rubber gloves and singing Moon River. All weapons must be checked! It is a good idea to mention what you are carrying and even have a picture handy to show. I myself packed a BSG sidearm and a Michael Myers butcher knife in my checked baggage and had no trouble at all. As a side note, I did carry two lightsabers as carry on, and I DID make it through, but believe me, they took a good hard look at them! Another piece of advice. Do not over pack! Hauling six bags of luggage is something you DO NOT want to do! More on this later when I get to the elevators.

If you are driving this makes it a little easier to carry more and be less cautious about weaponry but remember that parking when you get to Atlanta, can be costly. Hotels range from $25 – 40 or more a night. It is also a good idea to plan your route well. Atlanta moves bloody fast and last second merging is not a fun game of pole position.

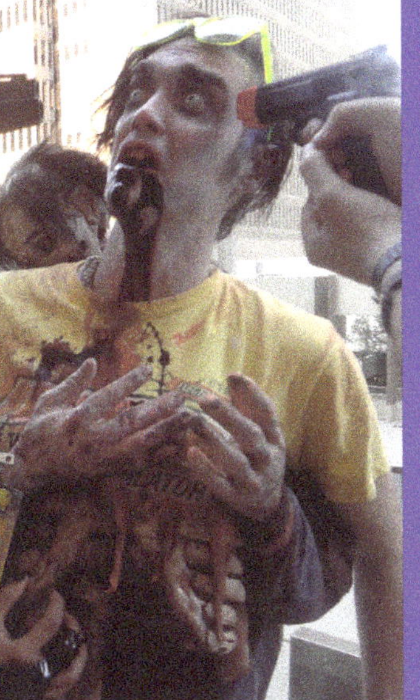

Now that you are there and doubtlessly enjoying the "Pie" you need a place to crash! And hotels sell out almost a YEAR in advance! You want to jump on this the moment you get home from the last one if not sooner or you could wind up in a hotel at the airport IF you are lucky! I am telling you… Do. Not. Wait. However if you choose not to heed this advice, hopefully one of your friends did and you can score an inflatable mattress (Bows to our Khaleesi whom was kind enough to share her room with us last time). And a shameless shout out to Jessika Sheogorath, ONI DUH GOD, Robert, Caine, Scarlett and Luna, my roomies last year!

So now you have arrived! Disheveled and travel worn. What should you do now? Get some sleep right? WRONG! Don't count on that for a few days. Perhaps a drunken pass out or a nap here and there but consider yourself Radu from Subspecies (and by the end of Con you may look like him whether male or female). Oh and start taking airborne and vitamins now. More on that later because I am getting ahead of myself.

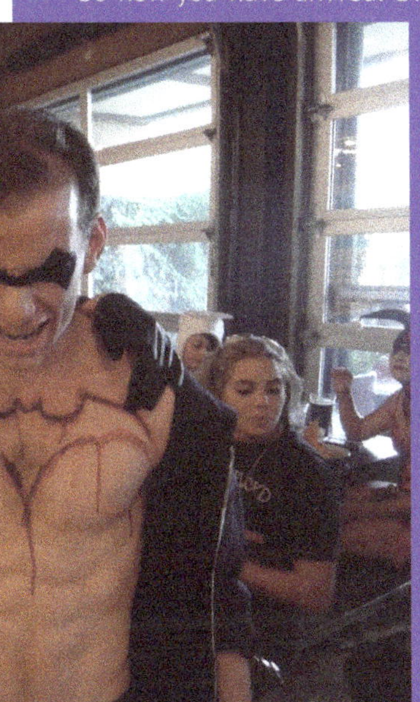

Thursday is the new Friday so they say and Con has already begun as far as smaller events and room parties. So get to the host hotels!

A word on "pie". This is a DragonCon unofficial tradition. Pie is a

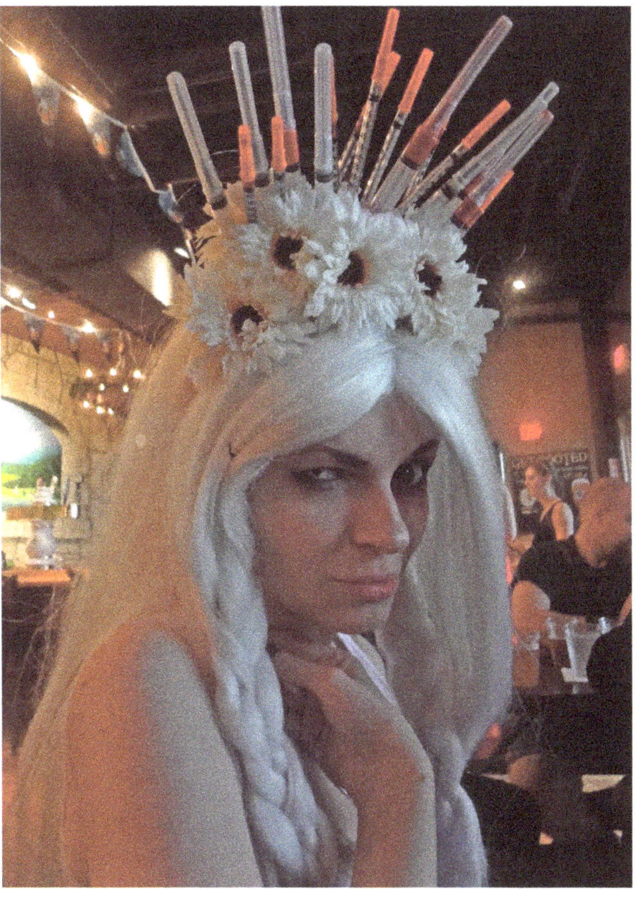

powerful drink and home made. So when you drink it, you never experience the same thing twice. The long time brewers of this fine potion have got it down to a science, and if it is done right it tastes exactly like the apple pie your momma used to make in autumn. Or at least like the warm crispy ones from MacDonald's. It may taste sweet and wonderful, but take it easy on the first night because it is stronger than it tastes. Unless you want Bob and Carl the Sci-Fi Janitors to be sweeping up your passed out corpse on the Marriott carpet the next morning.

So, now you have arrived and Con has truly begun with the rise of Friday morning dawn! Time to begin! First order of business (even better to do on Thursday) is getting your badge! If you ordered ahead of time then make sure to bring your postcard. If you are buying at the door don't forget your ID. Follow the colored path to your badge! Some will tell you one-way or the other (pre-order vs. at the door) is faster. I have experienced both. However, ordering online well in advance is cheaper. Anyone notice a pattern yet?

Now, what to do? This is where I give you good and bad news. Unless you have a TARDIS or a Time Turner you will never be able to do all the things you want to do, but the good news is

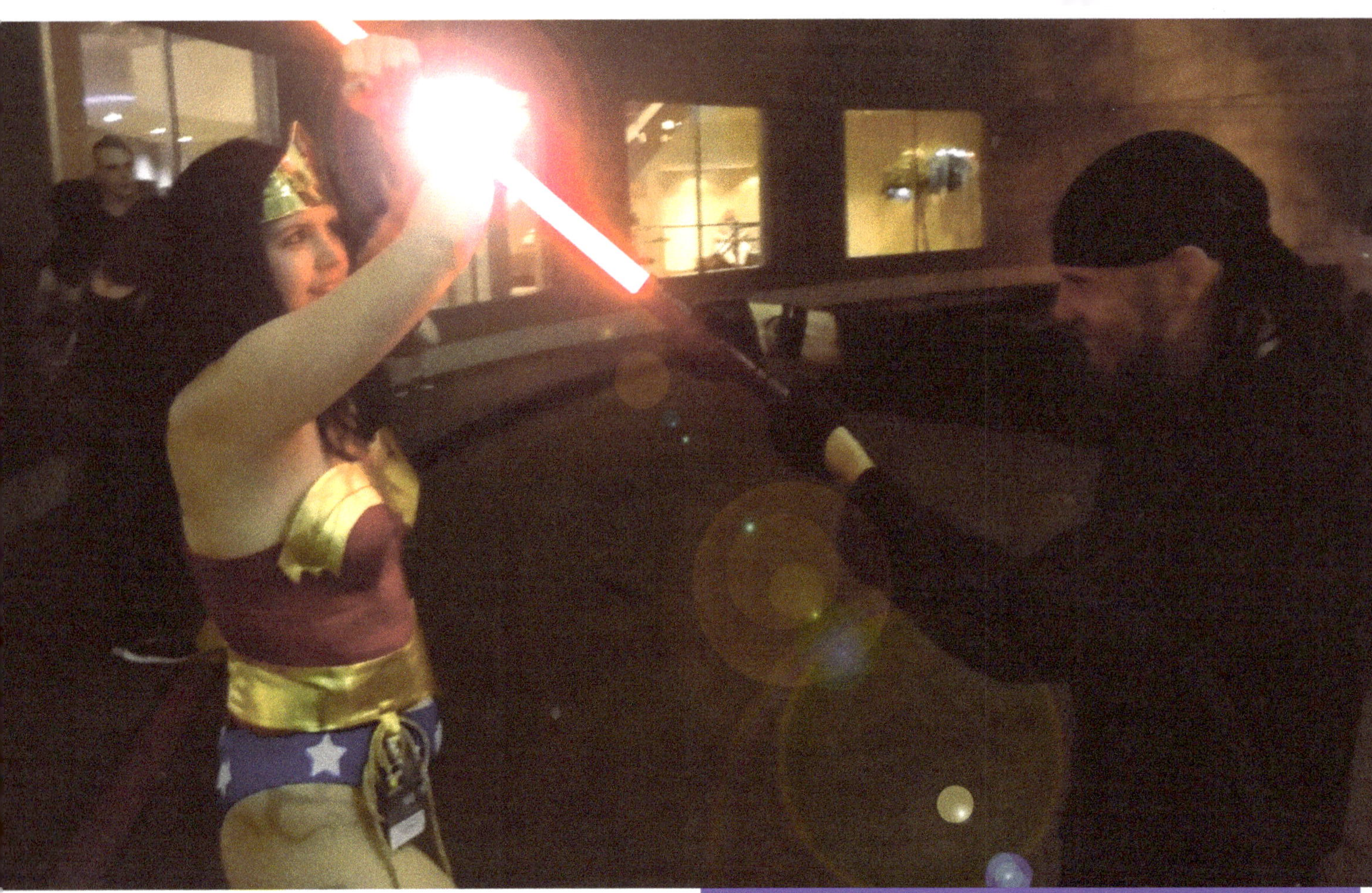

that there is SO MUCH to do that you will never be able to do everything you want to do! During the day there are a number of "tracks" to follow so pick your favorite! There are Anime, Art, British, Costuming, Fantasy, "Filk", Horror, Paranormal, Puppetry, Robotics, Space and the list goes on and on. Within each track are numerous Q &A's with celebrities, speaking engagements, demonstrations, workshops, photo ops and much much more. And this is only the beginning.

Ever wanted your own lightsaber? Or perhaps a phaser? What about a full belly dancing outfit or a sonic screwdriver? There are three massive dealer rooms with everything from used tattered old yellow comic books to the very props from the original Star Wars depending on your luck. Or perhaps you have always wanted to shake hands with one of the Hobbits from the Lord of the Rings? Or to get an autograph from Chewbacca? There is an entire hall of celebrities from a plethora of TV shows and movies where you can meet the stars. Be prepared to pay for autographs and taking photos depends on the guest. Many are happy to pose with you. Some however are not. There are also author rooms and artist rooms. Word to the wise though. If you hope to meet Terry Gilliam, William Shatner, Stan Lee or any other A-lister, then get there early!

And I mean really early. If you have not noticed my over all theme of expedience by now then you are doomed to the Hell of the Never Ending Elevator (but again more on that later).

When you pick up your badge, you can grab a con guide from the Seussian stacked boxes that are always nearby. That or down load the phone app. You are going to need it! Because again,

there is so much to do and so much happening all of the time. One small note on phones. With over 60 thousand people all on their phones, you can count on Wi-Fi being slow.

There are special events that take place every year. The Atlanta Aquarium holds a party one evening and full costumes are encouraged. This event grows in popularity every year.

If you are able to shamble like a walker out of your room early on Saturday, you will see one of the coolest parades ever! Divided into genres like Game of Thrones, Star Trek, and Battlestar Galactica, the parade is a tradition and one of the only places on Earth you will see a platoon of Stormtroopers walking down the street! I will say it one more time… Get there early or be prepared to scale a parking garage or light post in order to see.

A lot of the real excitement however occurs at night. Every night there are guest performances from a number of eclectic bands. An interesting fact. The majority tend to side on the Gothic range of musical taste. Amongst those whom have played I myself have seen Bella Morte, Ego Likeness, Spider Lilies, I:Scintialla, Ghoultown, Voltaire, Ayria and many others. The Cruxshadows are in fact a DragonCon tradition and play every year. After the live shows, dance parties, themed balls and room parties break out all over the many hotels. You may not sleep! It is DragonCon!

Of all the things I have listed here, believe it or not, these are only a part of what DragonCon has to offer. The list goes on for days. But I have not yet finished with my advice!

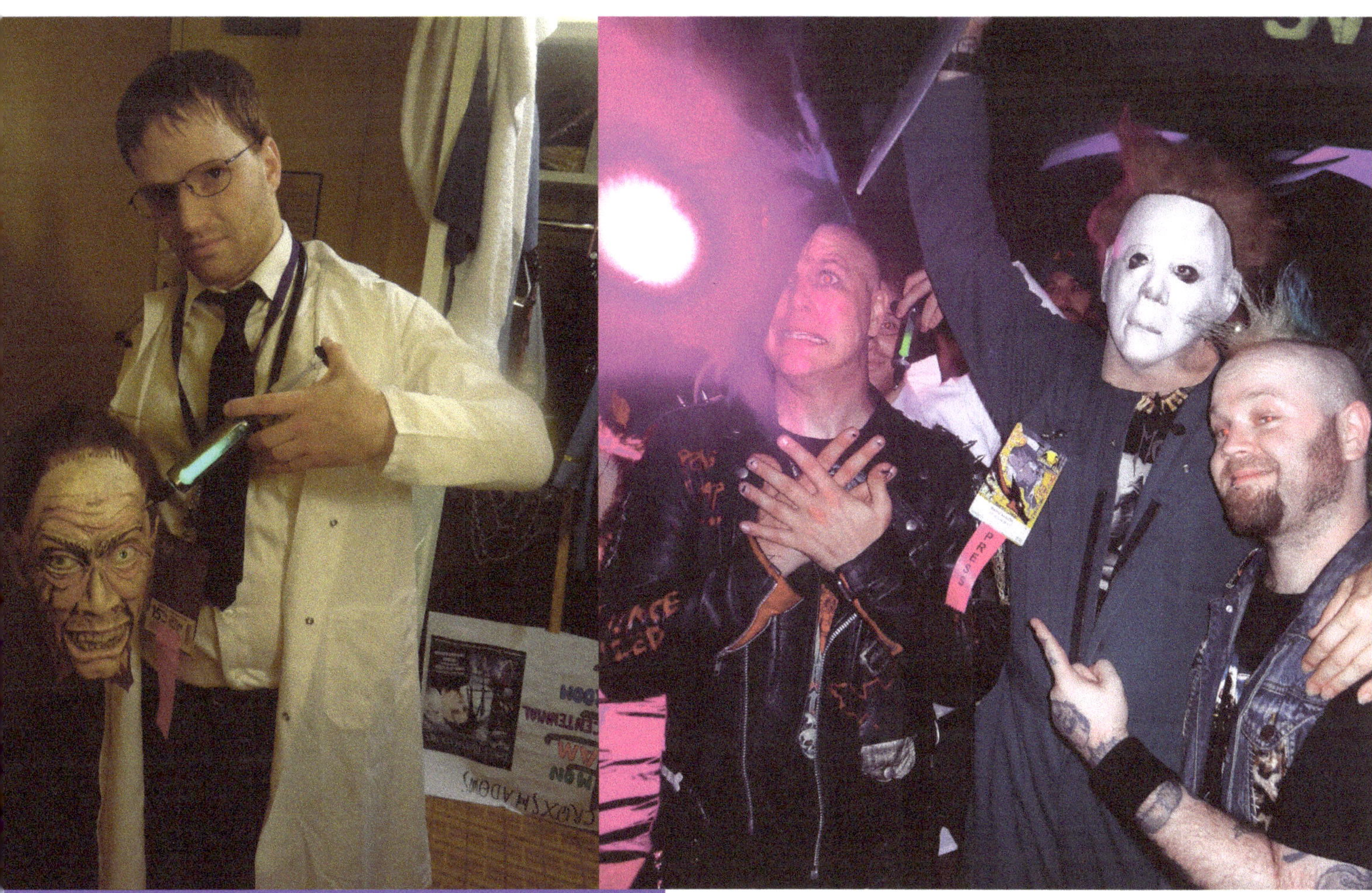

The Elevators… Welcome to Purgatory. Abandon Hope All Ye that must get to the 20th floor of the Marriott! The elevators in all of the host hotels are a study in patience and determination. At any given point they are packed so thick that birth control may be advised. A hint to surviving is that sometimes going down is going up and vice versa. In other words if you have the chance to jump on, JUMP ON! Even if it is going the wrong way. And speaking of sardines, welcome to the hallways and skywalks! Be prepared to take your time moving about because any enclosed space is generally packed! Be patient! And make new friends! They may be your travel companions for a few minutes.

And on that I return to the subject of vitamins. There is one thing almost everyone takes home with them other than a hangover and a con badge. This is the notorious CON CRUD. If you spend enough time around 60 thousand plus people, chances are you are going to catch something. It just happens. It is a part of the whole experience. However, you can stave it off if you strengthen your immune system beforehand and maintain it during the weekend. And while you are at it, remember you are in the south. If you are wearing Harry Potter robes, Stormtrooper armor, or a full Xenomorph exoskeleton then you must stay hydrated!

So now you have spent three days or more drinking, shopping, walking, dancing, moshing, drinking more, walking more, listening, standing in lines, pogo sticking, taking cabs, shopping again, posing on the concourse and probably having sex with a Klingon. Time to leave!

I'm not going to tell you to start early again. Those that must be told by now, have been damned to the con elevators. However, getting ahead on your packing is a good idea because if you didn't heed my advice about over packing then all the things you bought, all those rare collectibles or works of art or 8X10 autographed pics have to go somewhere! And if you are in a host hotel, trying to get your baggage down those elevators… see above.

There is one last thing. Another side effect of con is the withdrawal. You just had an amazing few days and now you must face life again. If you asked off from work I highly recommend that you ask off an extra day. You will want to decompress. New friends and old may be missed. Con Crud may be grabbing you. Hangovers must be slept off and sleep in general may very well be desperately needed. Take the time to recover. And then 24 hours later start getting on the phone, booking rooms for next year, and planning your costumes! Because as I and my friends and roomies from last year say…

DRAGONKHAAAAAAAAAAAAAAAAAAAAAAAAAAAAN!!!!

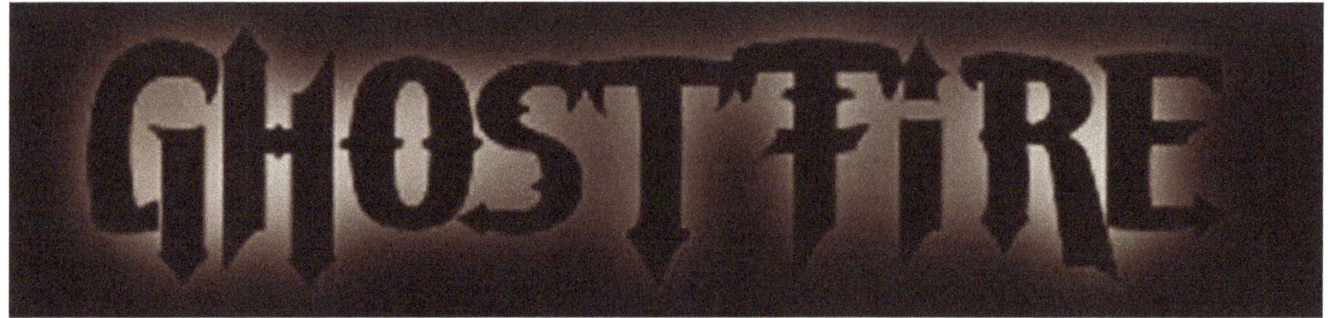

ALTERNATIVE FOLK, ROCK, STEAMPUNK

WATFORD, ENGLAND, UNITED KINGDOM

INDIE

By Kathleen Sharkey

The fog of early morn casts a pall on the dark alleys in the direst part of old London town. Through the dark miasma a hazy light blurs unbidden, like a dead man's lantern, haunting the darker shades of a forbidding Victorian era. It is from this misty staging that one would expect the gravelly Tom Waits like voice to beckon one to approach and take drink at a grungy alehouse and perhaps tell a tale or two about the darker side of a romantic era gone by. It is from this fundamental darkness that Ghostfire finds its poet's soul. Where many are looking to the romance and flights of fancy that the Steampunk movement finds so alluring Ghostfire reaches into the darkness and bring the shades of time gone by to life in the stories told in minor chord.

Begun in 2007 by Andii (guitar) and Al (drums), Ghostfire slowly but surely became home to a group of like-minded musicians looking for a place to produce music that represented their own country's history. By the time their first EP 'Drunk Lullabies' was released they had bumped the duo up to a five person band, knocking out amazing dark melodies. This was with the addition of Steven (vocals), Peter (bass) and swiftly acquired Rob (keyboards). Even with only two weeks to work together as a group it was well defined that this was going to work.

When Ghostfire's single "The Last Steampunk Waltz" was released in 2010 the band had significantly more rehearsal time together and a whole lot more performances. The sound of "The Last Steampunk Waltz" is definitely more cohesive and the dark flavor becomes more and more like the forbidden anise flavor of Absinthe. With no synthesizers (something very unique to this band), "Waltz" starts off with a music box waltz and then deep vocals flow in the tempo blending smoothly with harmonized backup vocals and a sprinkling of electric guitar. One wonders, in the story line of "Waltz" weather they are singing about England herself or some statue of a forgotten past watching the years fall by. "The Last Steampunk Waltz" was paired with "Hand of Glory" which sits as almost a polar opposite. "Hand of Glory", an even darker song then "Waltz", concerns a robber left to rot in the hangman's noose. Based upon a true practice of using a dead murderer's hand as a candle so that thieves could rob a house without being caught by its sleeping inhabitants. This song has a driving angry rhythm with almost a feel of 80's rock blended with Oingo Boingo goth but the storyline is all Ghostfire!

In 2011 Ghostfire released their first full length album "The Tyburn Jig and other Popular Dances".

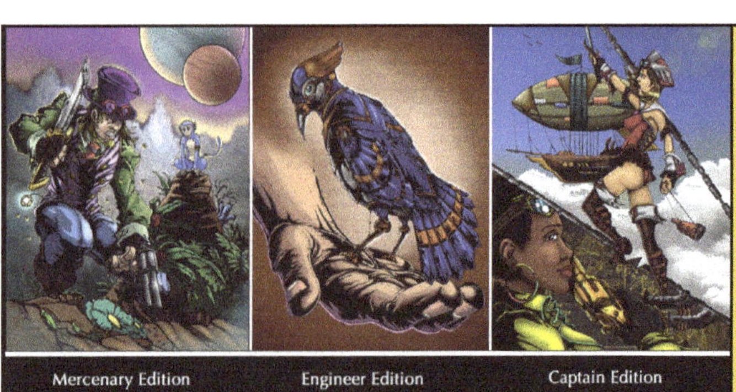

Mercenary Edition   Engineer Edition   Captain Edition

NEW LEGENDS:
MERCENARY • ENGINEER • CAPTAIN

A Steampunk Anthology
presented by Visual Adjectives!

HAPPY HAFFLAWEEN

Jezibell Anat

Darkness, darkness, recall the darkness, darkness, darkness, recall the might,
Darkness, darkness, it is our mother, darkness, darkness, we are the night.

The nights lengthen, the weather turns cool, and we approach the season of shadows. October is the favorite month of the year for those of us in the Gothic/alternative scenes. The rest of the year we are sometimes criticized for being too dark and intense and scary, but now it seems like everybody suddenly wants to play in our sandbox.

Historically, Halloween has both a solemn and a mischievous aspect. Halloween derived from the ancient Celtic holiday of Samhain, the final harvest celebration and the beginning of the long winter. This was the time of honoring the departed, when the souls of the dead were said to return to earth for one night. This could be an occasion of both joy and fear, where people would disguise themselves as skeletons or spirits to either party with the dead or to avoid being harmed by them, so it encompassed both solemn and mischievous aspects

Over centuries and countries, Samhain morphed into Halloween, All Hallows' Eve, the night before All Saints' Day (November 1), and All Souls' Day, the Christian holy days honoring the departed. In Mexico, this holiday fused with the native Aztec celebration to become Day of the Dead, which is becoming more widely celebrated in North America. Halloween itself is becoming more and more popular in a secular context, not just for children's trick-or-treating, but an occasion for adults to play. For those who are usually more reserved, it is a chance to throw off convention, indulge in masquerade, and release our darker selves.

This season in all its dimensions has become a rich source of inspiration for artists, and belly dancers have shimmied in. Belly dance in the West has always contained a strong element of fantasy, drawing us into a magical world of genies and gypsies, exotic allure and timeless sensuality. Even women who do not dance can enjoy putting on a belly dance costume for Halloween and relishing the glamour and mystery.

The Haflaween, a belly dance hafla with a Halloween theme, allows dancers to showcase the darker styles of belly dance and explore new options of costume, makeup and character. This is the time when the Gothic belly

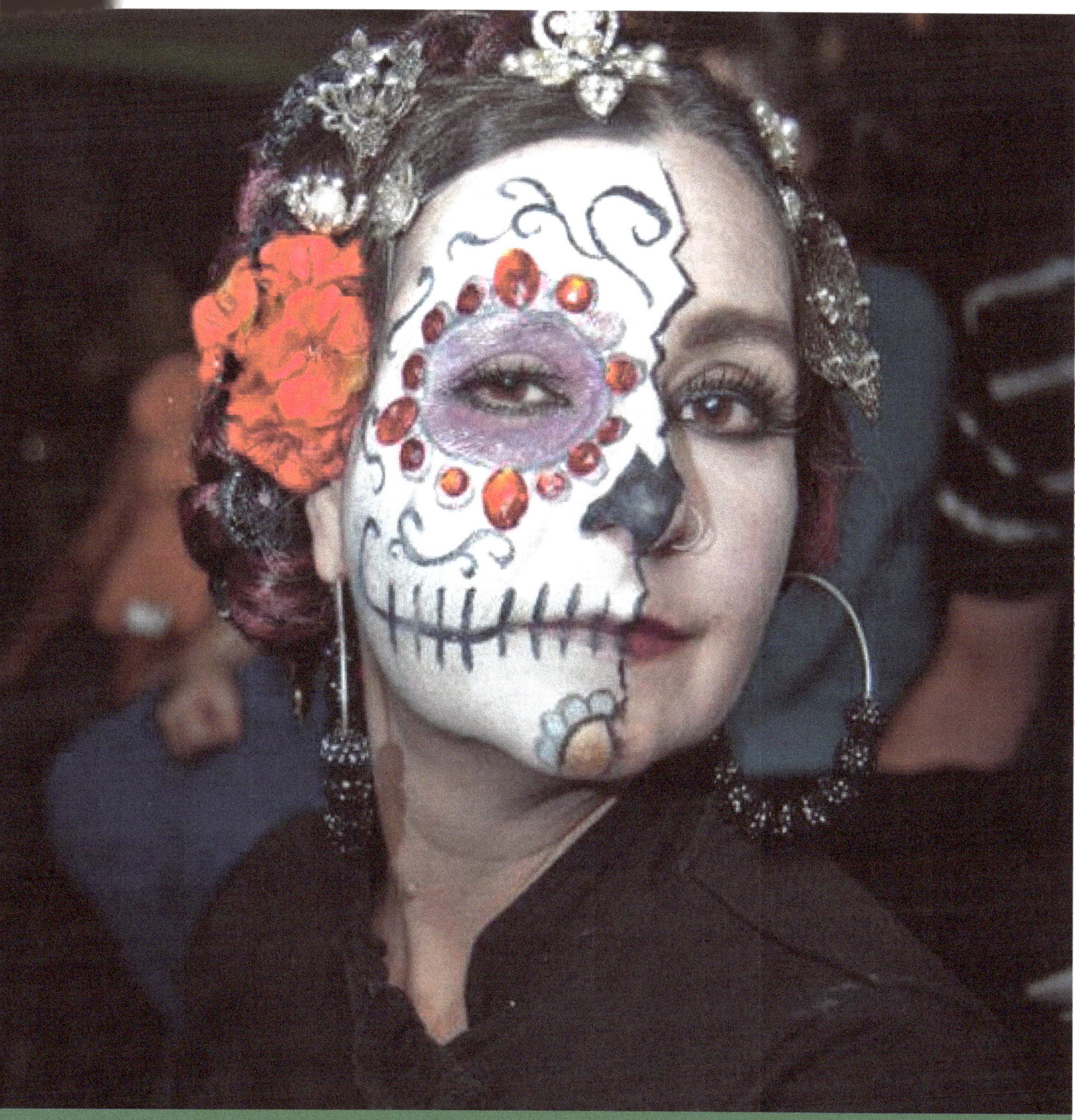

THE DARKER STYLES OF BELLYDANCE

dancer finds the most acceptance among the mainstream, and dancers who usually focus on traditional styles break out of their comfort zones and try something different.

The sad truth is that belly dancing still has a mixed reputation in many conservative parts of the country, even the modern styles that focus more on the elements of community, feminism, and empowerment, and there is some prejudice against the dancers who perform the dark alternative modes.

I have been told that some of my dances are too intense or too scary, especially my Kali Ma dance with Thai nails.

Belly dancing is entertainment, and audiences often expect the dancers to always be smiling and happy. But we dance to express emotion, and when we open our physicality to the music, the full depth of our feelings comes forth in all its variety. Our anger, our sadness, our desire, all these shadow selves of ourselves which we often keep hidden, may initially be

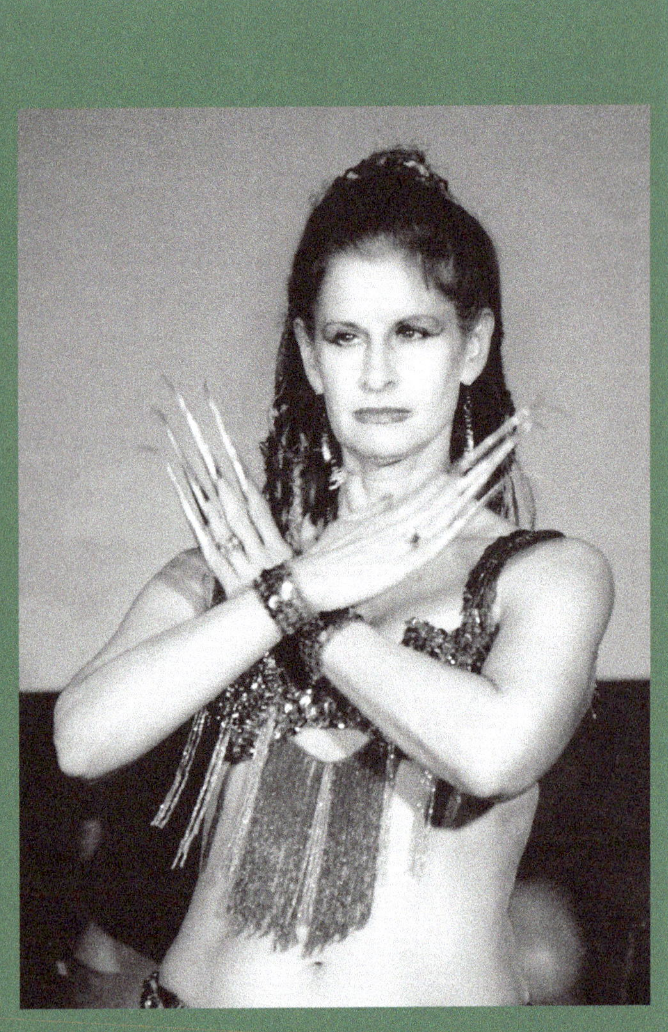

challenging for an audience. But for Haflaween the audience does not expect or even want a typical show, and emotions that might be uncomfortable from a cute, flirty dancer are appropriate for a mournful vampire or an angry banshee.

Pagan belly dancers often incorporate the spirituality of Samhain into their dances. Celtic scholar Alexei Kondratiev writes in The Apple Branch, "all true growth takes place in darkness: the source of vitality is in the unconscious, before the conscious discovers the limiting forms of rationality. Seeds sprout underground, away from the Sun. A child takes shape secretly in the lightless world of the womb, and is fully formed when born." Dancers may portray aspects of the Dark Goddesses, such as Ereshkigal, the Queen of the Underworld, or Hekate, Goddess of Witches.

Others take the chance to play, and zombies, femme fatales, ghosts, fairies, witches, psycho killers and many more take the stage. Freed from the need to always be pretty and pleasing, we make claw hands and grimaces and jerky monster moves and embody our characters. So Haflaween allows dancers to expand and explore their range and their power, bringing new dimensions to their presentations.

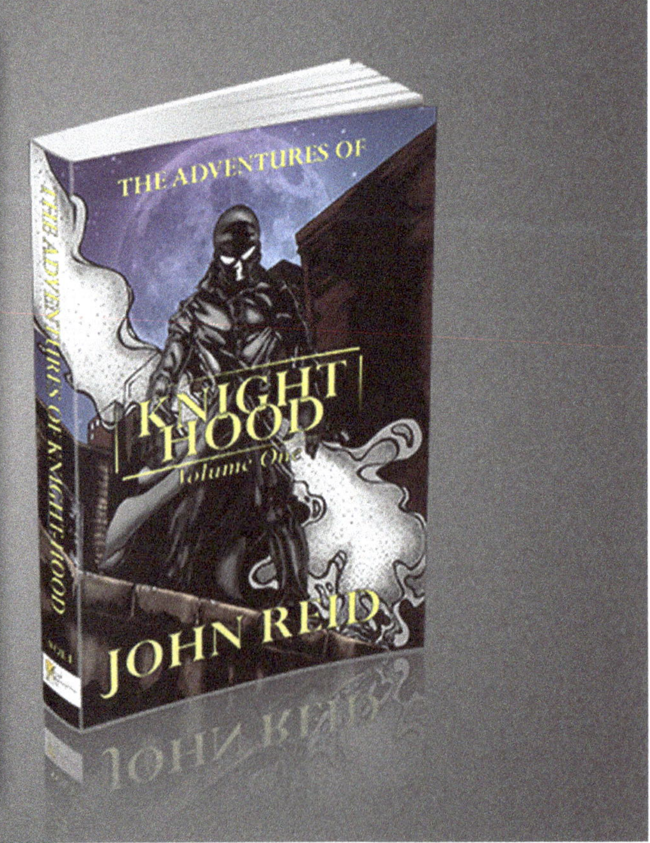

The Adventures of Knight-Hood: Volume I

Available on Amazon
Paperback $14.95
Kindle Price $2.99

What would you do if you lost everything, and found out you were going to lose your life as well?

Fed up with crime and injustice, Alex Breydon finds himself in such a position. No one has super powers. There are no such things as alien threats, and people do not possess magical abilities.

This is real life.

Alex decides, with nothing else to lose, he is going to fight the evils he sees occurring every day. Donning a mask and taking advantage of the technology available, he begins his crusade against crime. A "Knight in shining armor", who aids those in distress, he becomes, Knight-Hood. A Real Life Super Hero.

Why do we dress up at this time of year?
Things are not as they might appear.
We love to pretend, and be what we're not,
Beyond the limits of rule and thought.

For some, this is simply a chance to be merry,
To go out and collect all the treats they can carry.
But these costumes are more than make-believe,
They are a part of the web we weave.

The nights grow long, the wind blows cold,
And we celebrate a holiday that's very old.
When the leaves are turning to yellow and red.
It's Halloween, Samhain, Day of the Dead.

The summer is gone, the harvest is stored,
And we honor the ones who have gone before.
They have passed on, and their souls are freed,
So we remember their lives and their deeds.

And now, some believe that the dead return,
From tomb, from grave, from coffin and urn.
Perhaps as ghosts, perhaps as spirits,
A rustling in the wind for those who can hear it.

We decorate our altars to greet them,
We offer the bread and the salt as we meet them.
Our costumes and masks are more than a game,
As we share their memories and speak their names.

Once people would dress as the spirits of night,
As ghosts and skeletons by candle light
First to guide the dead on their way,
And then for merriment and play.
For when the dead return to the earth,
It's a time for reverence, a time for mirth.
And we still hold them in our hearts.
Even though they must depart.

And we can remember the people we knew,
As they enter the gate that we all pass through,
But we can respond with love, not fear,
And so we dress up at this time of year.

Jezibell Anat

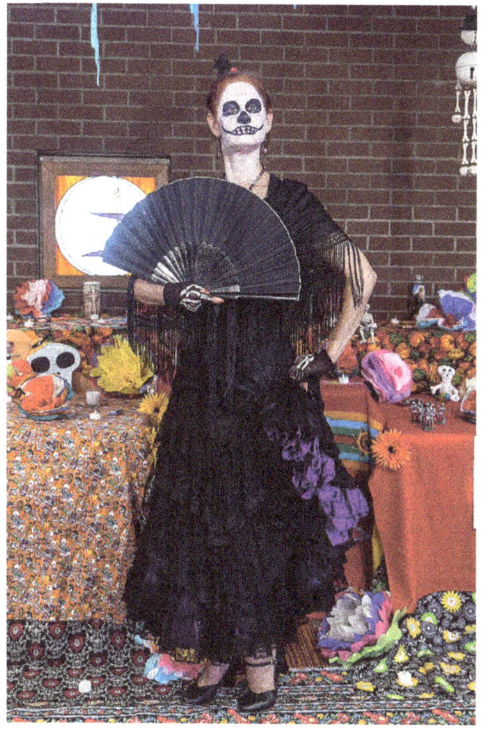

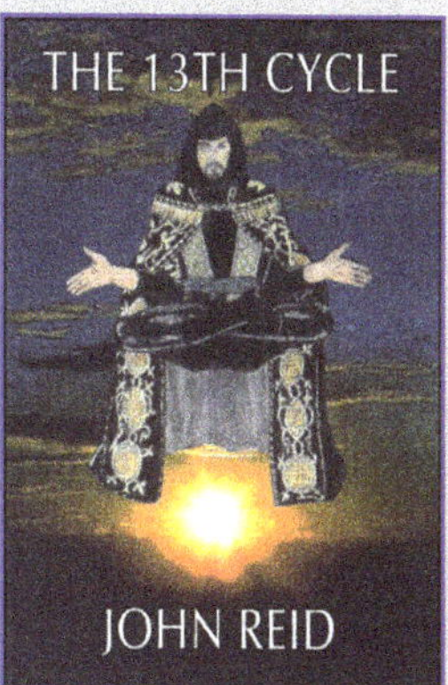

The 13th Cycle

When magician Paul Mathewson
was 13 years old he became
possessed by the spirit of Biblical
sorcerer Simon Magus. Magicians
label him a fraud and the Christian
fundamentalists declare him to be
the Anti-Christ. Even Paul begins
to wonder about that as he begins
to piece together the prophecies
of Nostradamus, the Book of
Revelations and Mayan prophecy.

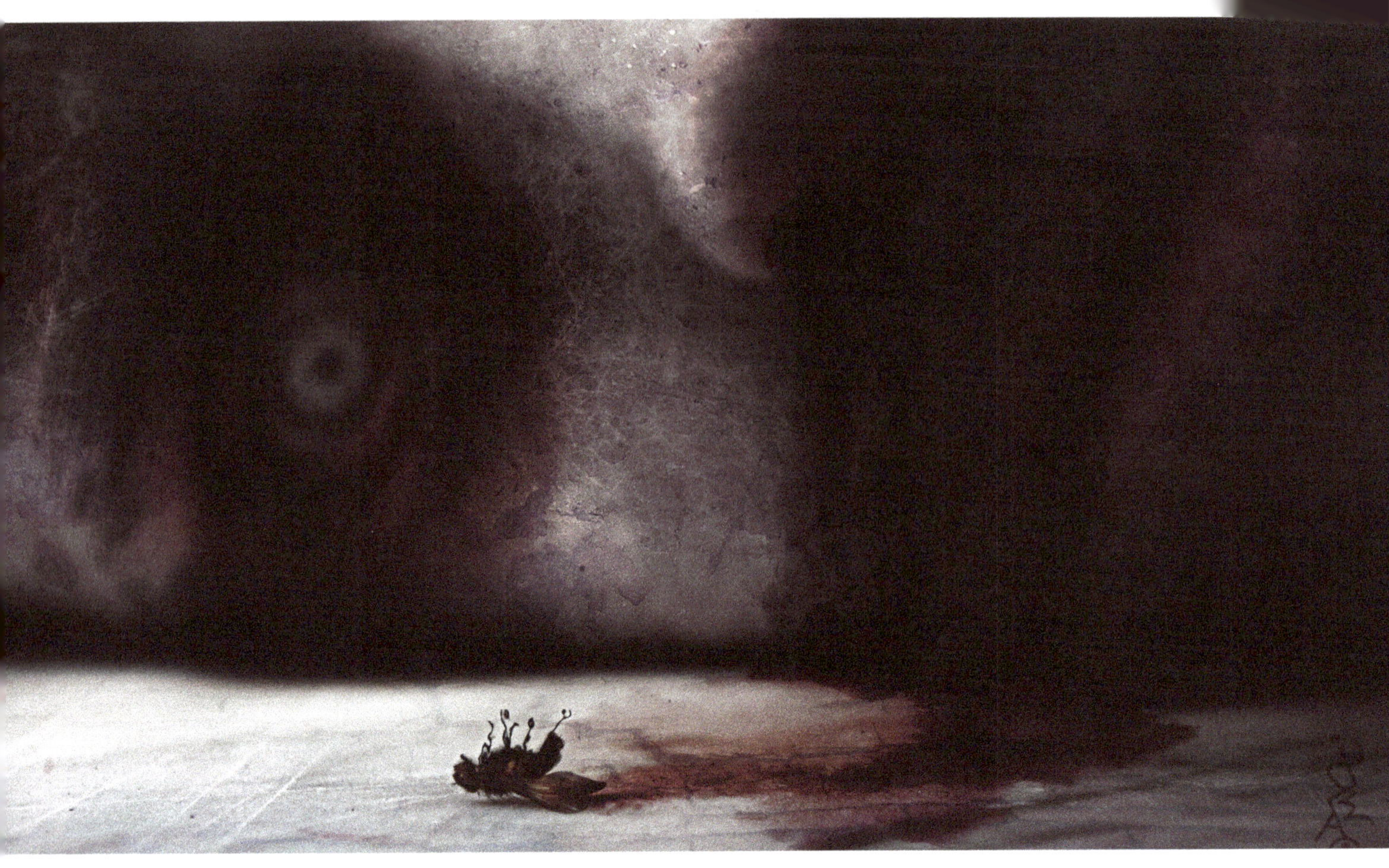

LUMINOUS DARKNESS

Armando Liccardo's intermediate spaces of the soul.

[Carpe Nocturne] Tell us, what type of art do you enjoy being involved in?

[Armando Liccardo] I really like every form of art and I like [to] explore and experiment with [them]. Today I'm taking photos, photo manipulating some of them, painting, drawing and writing, but I would sculpt and work with everything [that] can be transformed by my thought in hands.

[Carpe Nocturne] How long have you been involved in the Arts?

[Armando Liccardo] I have been involved in art since I was a child. I was very good at to reproducing by pencil the world [as] I saw it.

As I grew up I was looking for other ways to penetrate in the intermediate spaces of my soul and show it by the attitude of that time. Then [one] day I discovered Photography due to my father's old passion, and then Photoshop, and I began to work with both to get a way to my depth. Some time after I needed to write; I love writing, so my works are almost always followed by some written thoughts, or explanation et simili. In these days I'm exploring Painting, just another way to show the depth of my body/mind. Each kind of art i'm involved in gives me something different, they follow my moods. I realize that some of my thoughts come out better as photo, or painting, or photomanipulation, or a poem, or a drawing... and I realize that they can be combined to get a higher level of vision.

I like the preparation of the scene and then its manipulation.

[Carpe Nocturne] Who/What inspired you to get into Art/Photography?

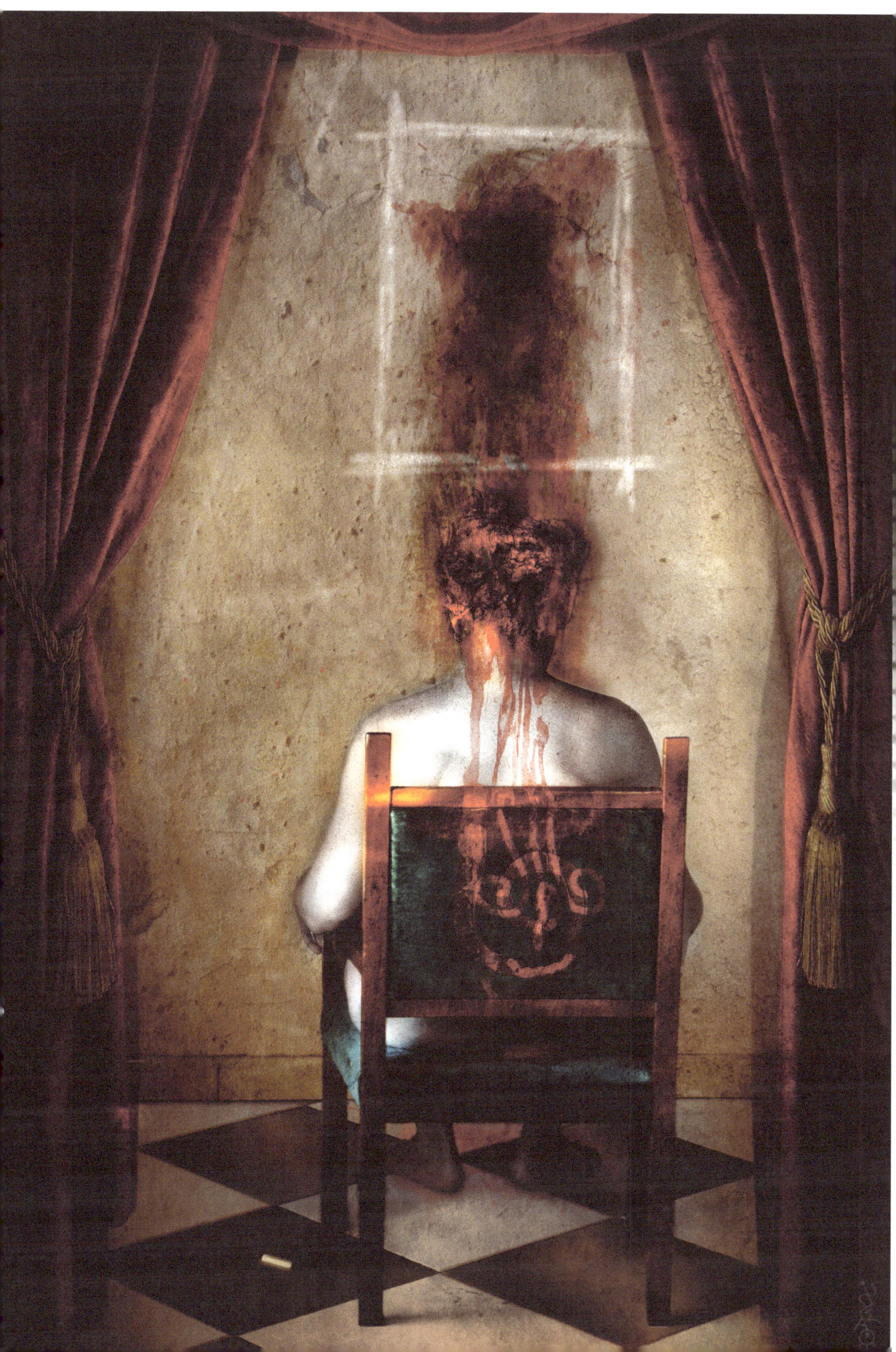

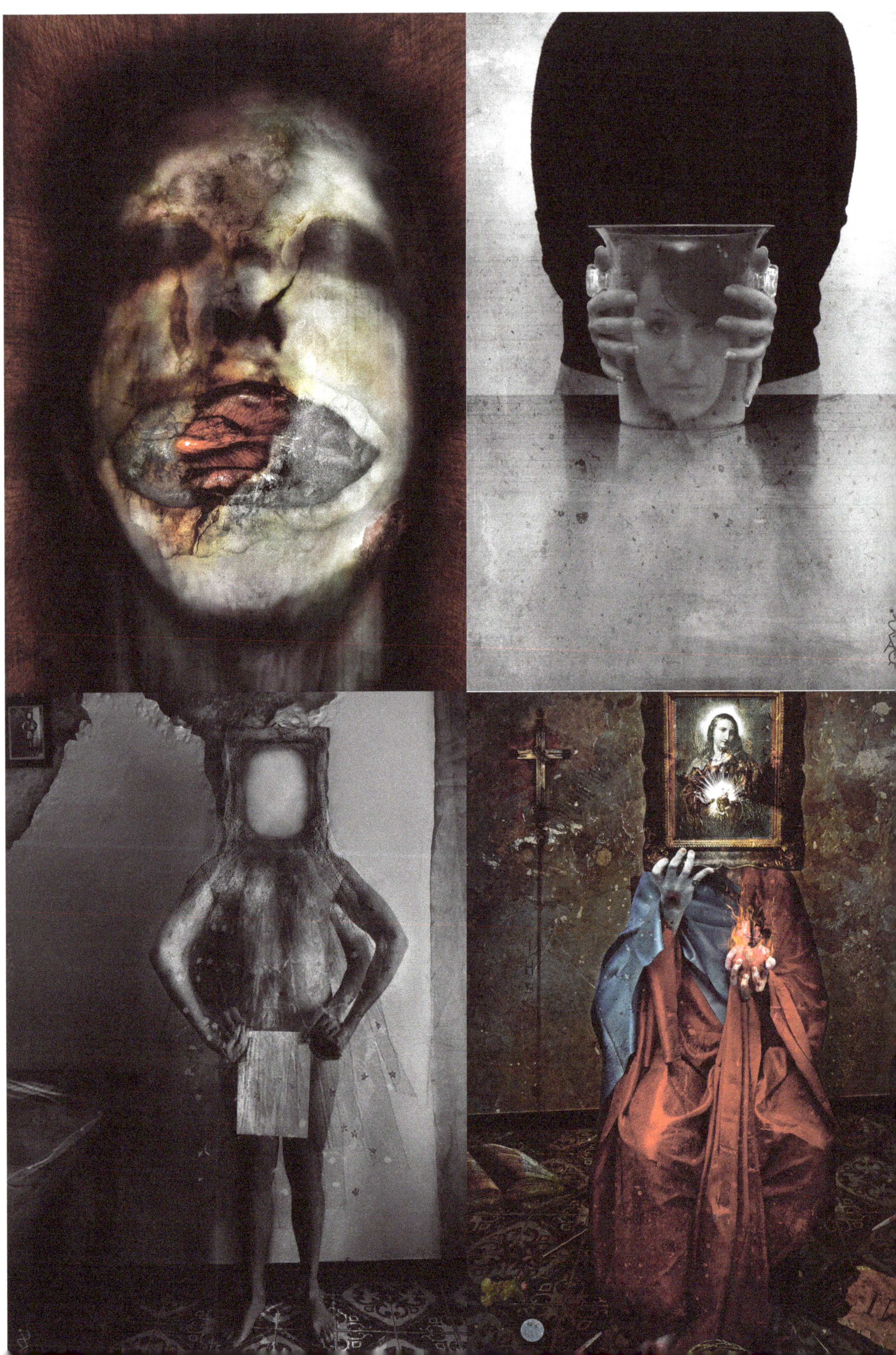

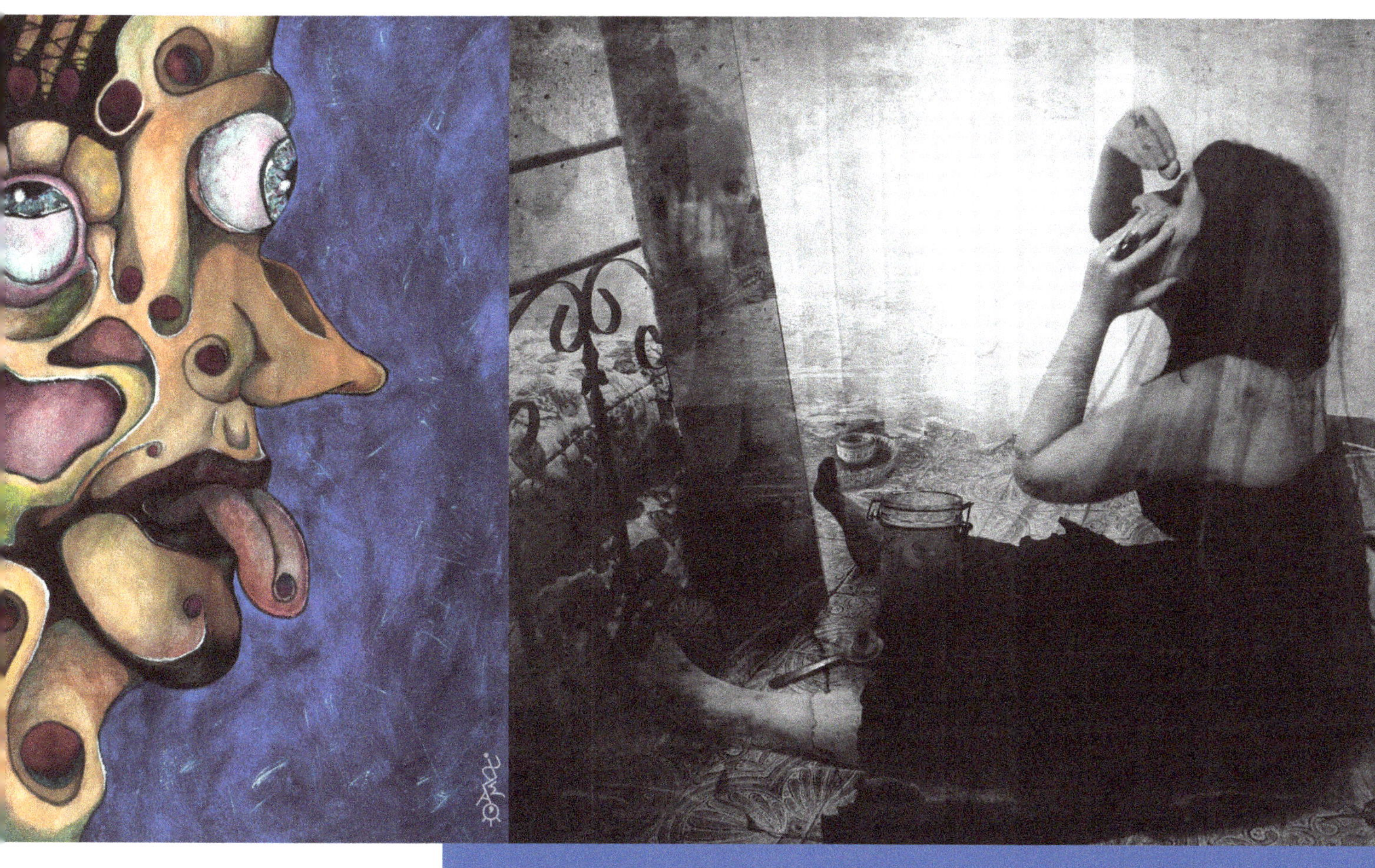

> **"**
> *Almost the totality of all my works are sort of visions, or dreams/nightmares, or sudden images I try to explore and show."*

[Armando Liccardo] I really don't know, I suppose the strong will to get out something screaming inside me.

[Carpe Nocturne] Are there any Artists who inspire you today?

[Armando Liccardo] I love the Viennese Actionism, Joel Peter Witkin, Dadaists, Surrealists and many others, but I don't know if they inspire me, for sure they opened my mind and now I'm in.

[Carpe Nocturne] Do You Have Any Schooling/Training In The Arts?

[Armando Liccardo] Nope. Everything I know about Photography, Photoshop, and Painting comes from my personal study or experiments. I'm self-taught.

[Carpe Nocturne] What Is your Favorite Subject?

[Armando Liccardo] My whole being and its link with everything. Almost the totality all of my works are sort of visions, or dreams/nightmares, or sudden images I try to explore and show. The subject of all of this is the void and its luminous darkness. The images, or visions, or dreams, can be landscapes, people, concepts, and so on, everything is a luminous moment of the void. Sometimes my works are murky to me too. I discover their symbolism and meaning only some time after.

[Carpe Nocturne] Is your work compared to the work of anyone else?

[Armando Liccardo] Maybe yes, maybe not, I don't know, I make my works.

[Carpe Nocturne] Do You Sell/Show Your Work At Any Galleries?

[Armando Liccardo] In this moment I don't sell my works but I could. I'll show my works in an Italian Art Gallery, after I became Artist of the Month for their web project.

KEEP CALM AND SHIMMY ON

By Isolde de Mortimer

You take classes and workshops and practice endlessly to perfect your technique and develop your personal dance style. Whether you perform once a year at your teacher's holiday hafla or hope to make bellydance your career, at some point in addition to all the rehearsing, you'll need to pack and prep for your performance. Here are a few tips to get you ready and keep you calm so you can shimmy on!

MAKEUP TIPS

☐ Wear lipstick instead of gloss to help prevent your hair from sticking to your lips during spins and turns.

☐ Unless you're performing at an outdoor venue, avoid makeup with sunscreen. It can oddly reflect lighting.

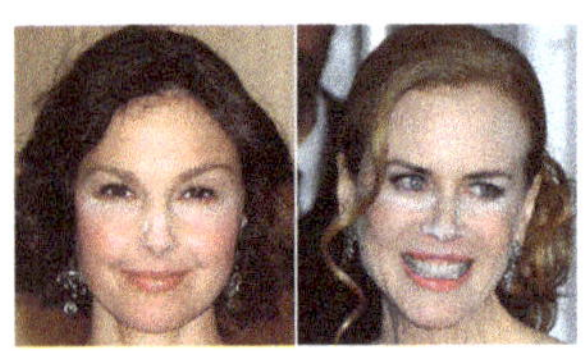

☐ Similarly, avoid or use silica powder sparingly. If not layered or blended properly, it can appear flawless in the mirror but look messy from flash photography.

☐ Take a straw for sipping your drink to save your lipstick.

☐ Pack a cotton ball in compacts to protect pressed makeup from cracking during transport.

☐ Makeup for more intimate gigs is about one and a half times more intense than your evening makeup.

☐ Stage makeup uses the same techniques as gig makeup but with a heavier hand. Darker, brighter colors, fuller lashes, and more glitter to emphasize angles and highlights.

☐ For stage, extend your liner and brows, even up to a centimeter, to make your features more prominent.

☐ Add loose cosmetic glitter to clear polish, lip gloss and body lotion to fully coordinate your look.

COSTUMING TIPS

☐ Before wear, scuff the bottom of new dance shoes with sandpaper, an emery board, even on concrete to avoid slipping.

☐ Pack a sewing kit, with needles threaded both with dark and light threads.

☐ Organize bangles on carabiner clips.

☐ Snap a quick selfie to check your makeup under flash and how your costume and hair look from another angle.

☐ For costuming on a tight budget, buy a bra and belt set in silver or gold which will coordinate with many skirt and harem pants colors.

☐ Inspect stones and links in new costume jewelry. Use pliers to tighten links and E6000 glue to replace loose stones.

☐ Use a coat of clear nail polish on the back of new costume jewelry to prevent contact with sweat and the resulting skin discoloration.

☐ Examine jewelry after each wearing and clean with a soft cloth.

☐ Compile a master packing list for gigs including emergency fixes such as extra pairs of stockings, safety pins, and baby wipes.

☐ Sew a small bead or knot of thread onto the elastic of your thumb zills for quick identification.

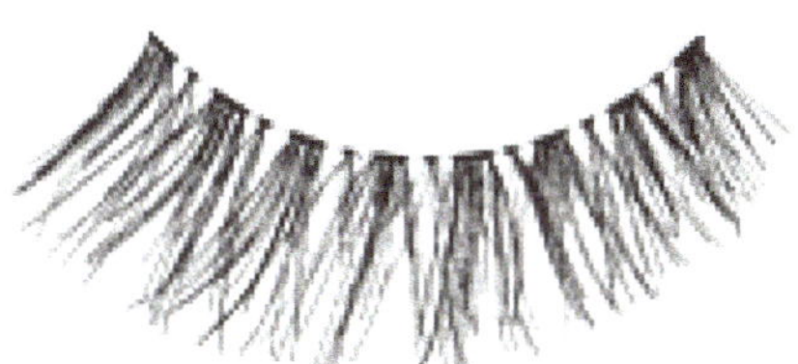

GIG LASHES

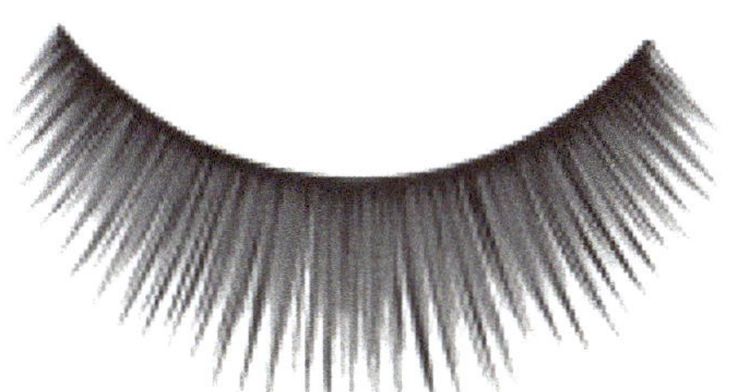

STAGE LASHES

CARBINE CLIP

REPAIR TIPS

- To retune zills, remove elastic and bake in oven for 20 minutes at 375 degrees. Then cool on a towel and replace elastic.

- Use clear nail polish to stop a run in stockings.

- Use baby wipes to freshen, clean up makeup messes, and spot clean costumes.

- To save your broken lipsticks either carefully soften the broken end still fixed in the tube with a lighter or match and gently press together with the broken end of the detached piece to fuse or scoop out all the lip color from the tube, place scrapings and the broken piece in a lip gloss pot, heat with a hair dryer to melt into place, and allow to set.

- Fix shattered pressed makeup by crushing up all the pieces, adding rubbing alcohol until it has a creamy consistency, smoothing the top, and letting dry.

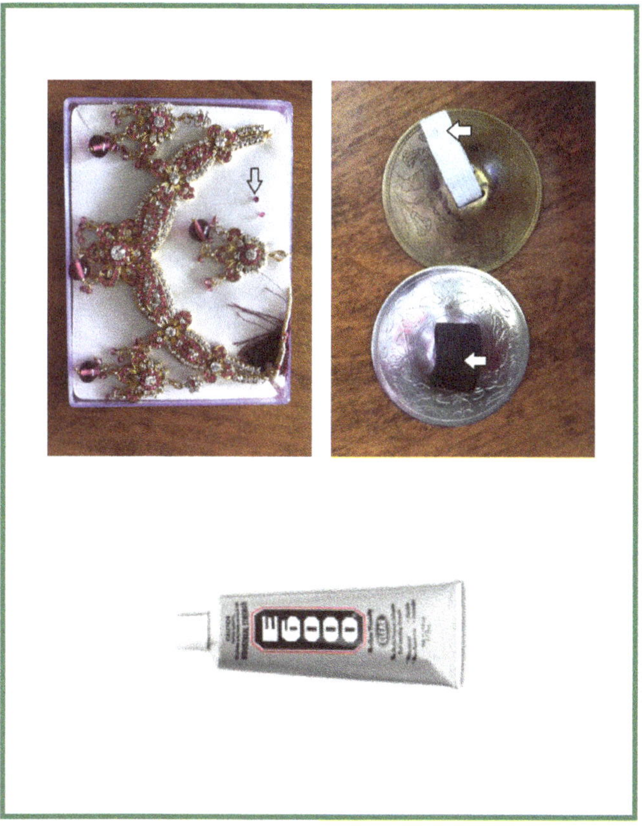

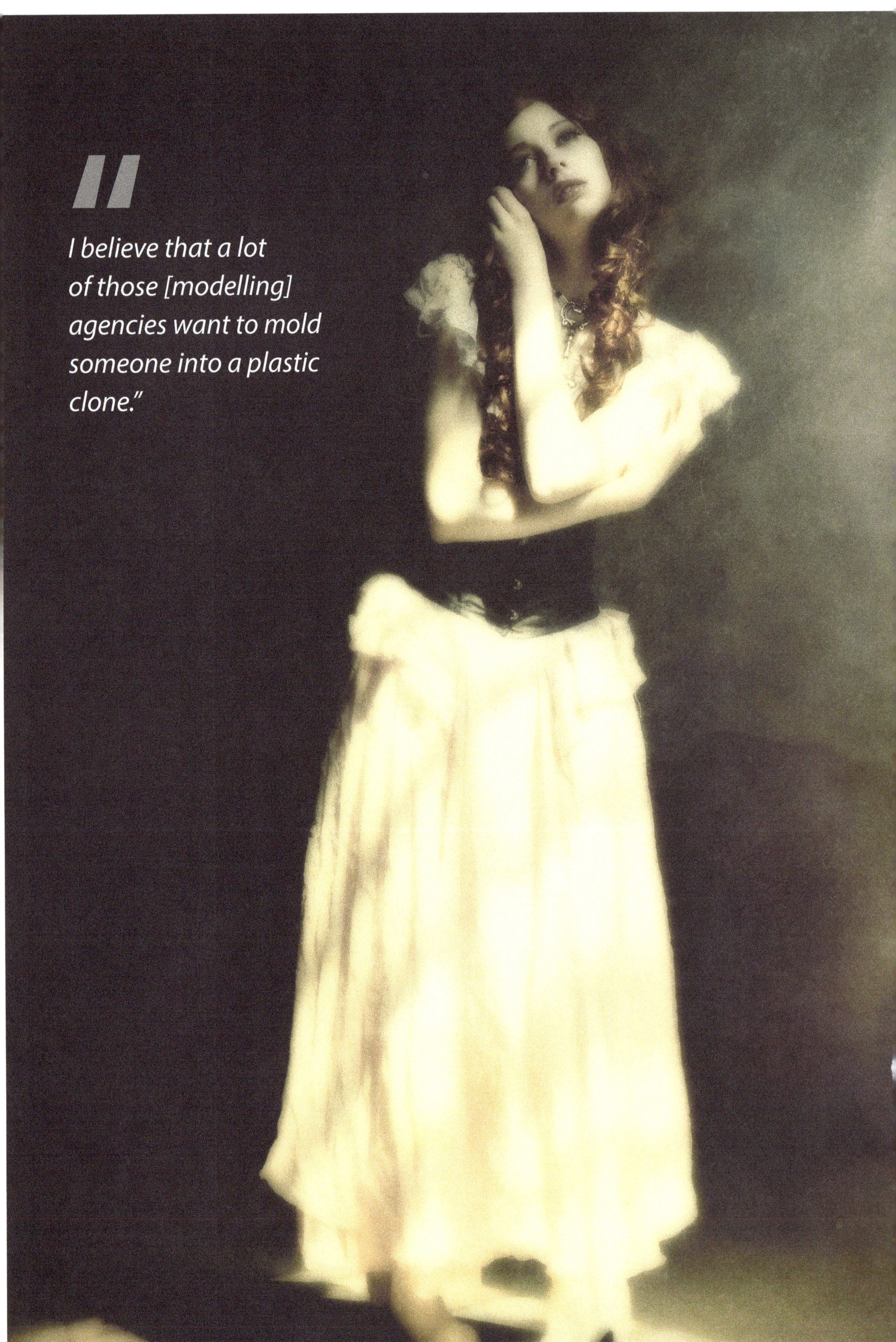
"
I believe that a lot
of those [modelling]
agencies want to mold
someone into a plastic
clone."

OPHELIA DARKLY
CELEBRATING UNIQUENESS

(Carpe Nocturne) So, tell us a little bit about yourself, Ophelia.

(Ophelia Darkly) I officially started modeling a little over two years ago, but I feel like I've been modeling and creating for a lot of my life. I say this because I was always interested in fashion and modeling, but I wasn't able to really start developing my own sense of style until high school when my extremely religious and conservative mother didn't have as much control over what I wore.

(Carpe Nocturne) What are some of the challenges you've faced in your modelling career?

(Ophelia Darkly) One of the biggest challenges I've had to overcome involves my physical appearance. For years I was told I was ugly and felt like I was. The primary reason I felt that way centers around a scar I have on my face. On the right side of my face is a crescent-shaped jagged scar from plastic surgery. I obtained this scar in only first grade from being bitten by a dog. After this event, I was often alienated. Even in high school, people would yell out that I had herpes. If anything, this traumatic event in my life pushed me even further towards alternative modeling and the alternative scene. I recall years ago (as in about 8 years) walking into Hot Topic when it wasn't as mainstream and seeing this guy clothed in black with spiked hair and two different coloured eyes. I was scared, excited, intrigued, and most of all, amazed. Ever since then, I've gotten more and more into alternative fashion and I started modeling. I currently live outside of Chicago and have been rejected by all the big fashion agencies! Even though I have "fashion stats," I believe that my scar has made it so that agencies do not want to sign me. Applying to them has really taught me a lot. I believe that a lot of those agencies want to mold someone into a plastic clone. They do not celebrate uniqueness. This is what has drawn me to alternative modeling. I feel that I am being myself. I'm not putting on a costume to take a photograph. This is who I am.

(Carpe Nocturne) Are You Involved In The Scene At All?

(Ophelia Darkly) Definitely! I'm so glad that I moved to the Chicago land area because before (I graduated from college recently) I had moved to Iowa

REFUSING THE FASHION INDUSTRY'S PLASTIC PARADIGM

Ophelia Darkly, an alternative fashion model, talks to us at Carpe Nocturne about her involvement with the scene and her modelling experiences.

Left: Photo by Dividing ME
Contents: Red Generation

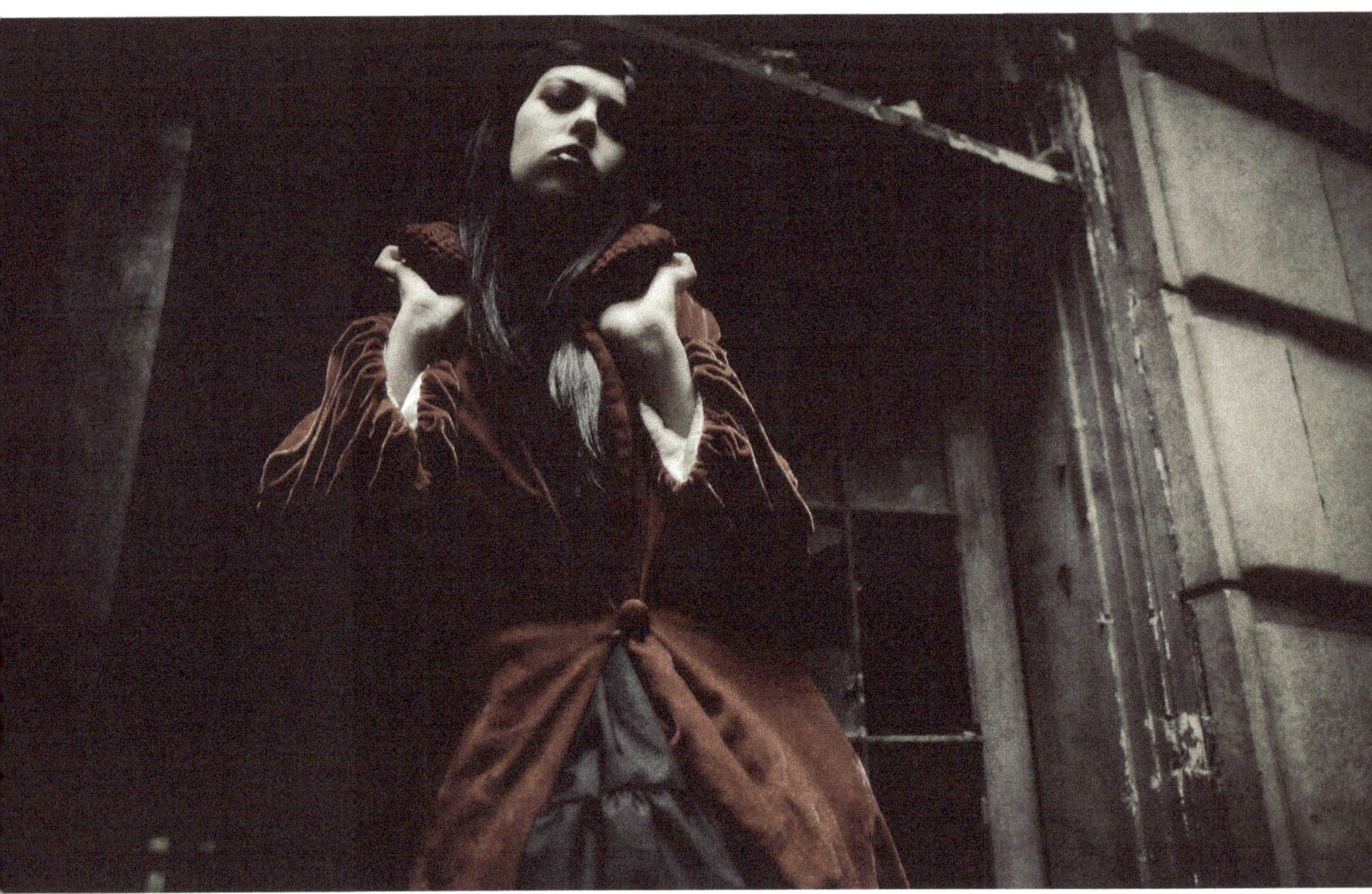

Top: Photo by Red Generation   **Right**: Photo by Dividing ME

for school. There is one gothic industrial club in Iowa and that's it (I actually met my fiancé there). I was often ridiculed for my appearance there. I absolutely love going to concerts and since my fiancé is an industrial musician, I am exposed to a lot of great music. I think music is such an important part of "the scene". I also, of course, love the fashion and enjoy going to stores in Chicago like The Alley and Beatnix as they support the alternative lifestyle. In addition to that, I absolutely love to dance, so I love clubbing! We have an excellent event at the Metro here called Nocturna hosted by Scary Lady Sarah. When I go to events like this, I no longer feel isolated. I feel such a sense of community.

(Carpe Nocturne) Tell Our Readers About Your Interests, Likes and Dislikes.

(Ophelia Darkly) This list could go on an on! I'll just start with my dislikes. I dislike: ignorance, overtly religious people who shove their views in your face, strawberry milk, black licorice, big dogs, spiders, people who are conceited and or stupid, rap and country music, driving, perverts, winter, fake tans, pornography, hospitals, my paranoia. I like/love: dreads, my fiancé, music (too many bands to name), people who aren't afraid to be themselves, poetry, theatre, Shakespeare, clothes, shoes, bunnies (I have 2!), warm weather, books, Emily Dickinson, forests, people watching, wigs, vibrant makeup, parasols, corsets, butterflies, rocks, seashells, the movie The Hours, abandoned buildings, chocolate.

(Carpe Nocturne) What Do You Enjoy For Hobbies and Interests?

(Ophelia Darkly) I have many! Sewing clothes is one even though I usually don't use a pattern so it comes out looking sort of archaic, playing the piano, dance, acting, writing poetry, scaring normal looking people, and collecting things. My interests are pretty much in the 'like' section.

(Carpe Nocturne) Who Are Some Of Your Favorite Bands / Music, Artists, Movies?

(Ophelia Darkly) Top favorite bands: Christian Death, Gary Numan, God Module, Joy Division, Marilyn Manson, Michael X. Christian (my fiance's music), Nirvana, Pink Floyd (early years), Rammstein, Tori Amos, and The White Stripes. My favorite artist is Salvador Dali. Movies: Amelie, The Lovely Bones, The Hours, The Ring, The Breakfast Club, Eternal Sunshine of the Spotless Mind, Harry Potter series, The Others, Edward Scissorhands, Monty Python and the Holy Grail, American Beauty, Kill Bill, Atonement, and Girl Interrupted.

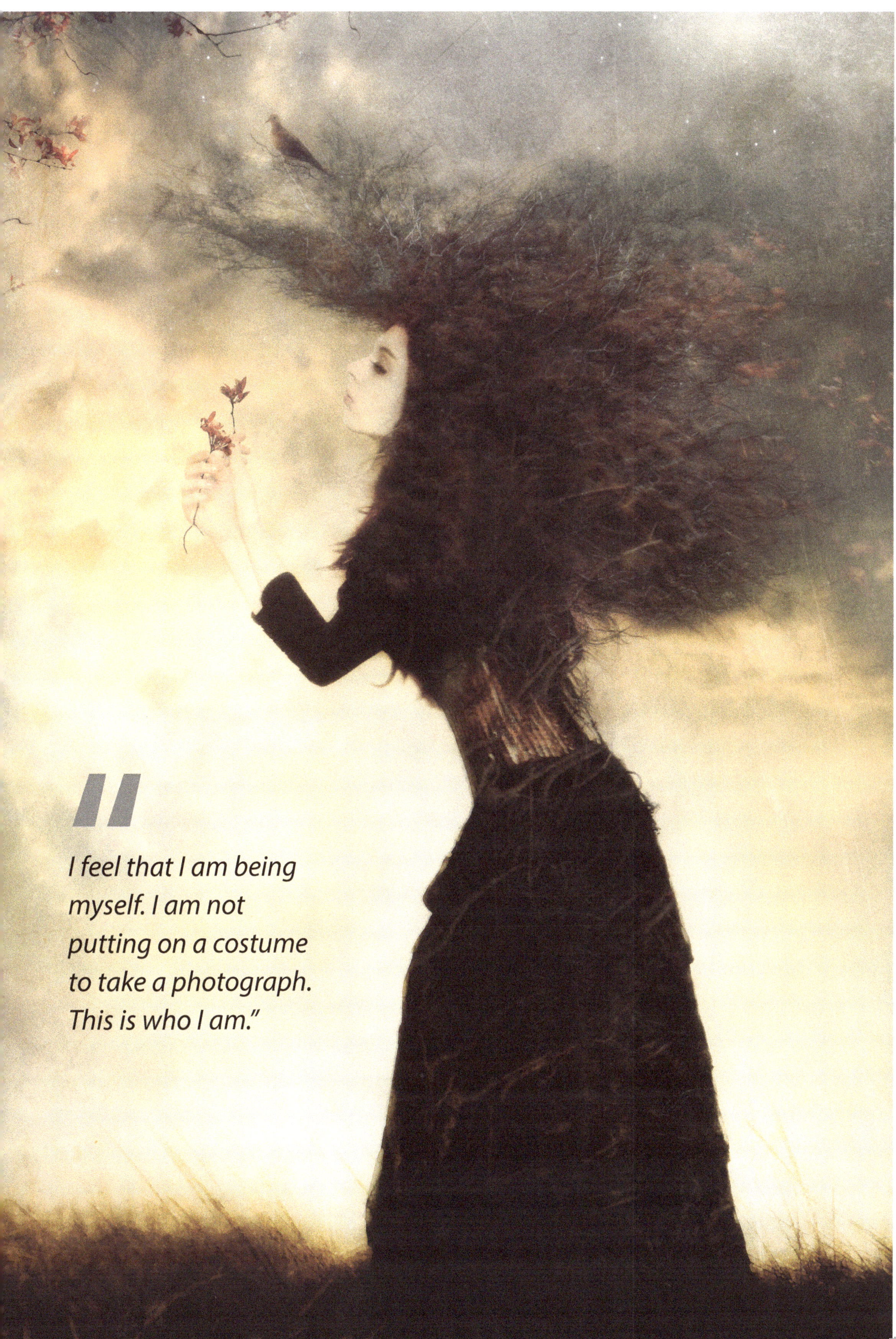
I feel that I am being myself. I am not putting on a costume to take a photograph. This is who I am."

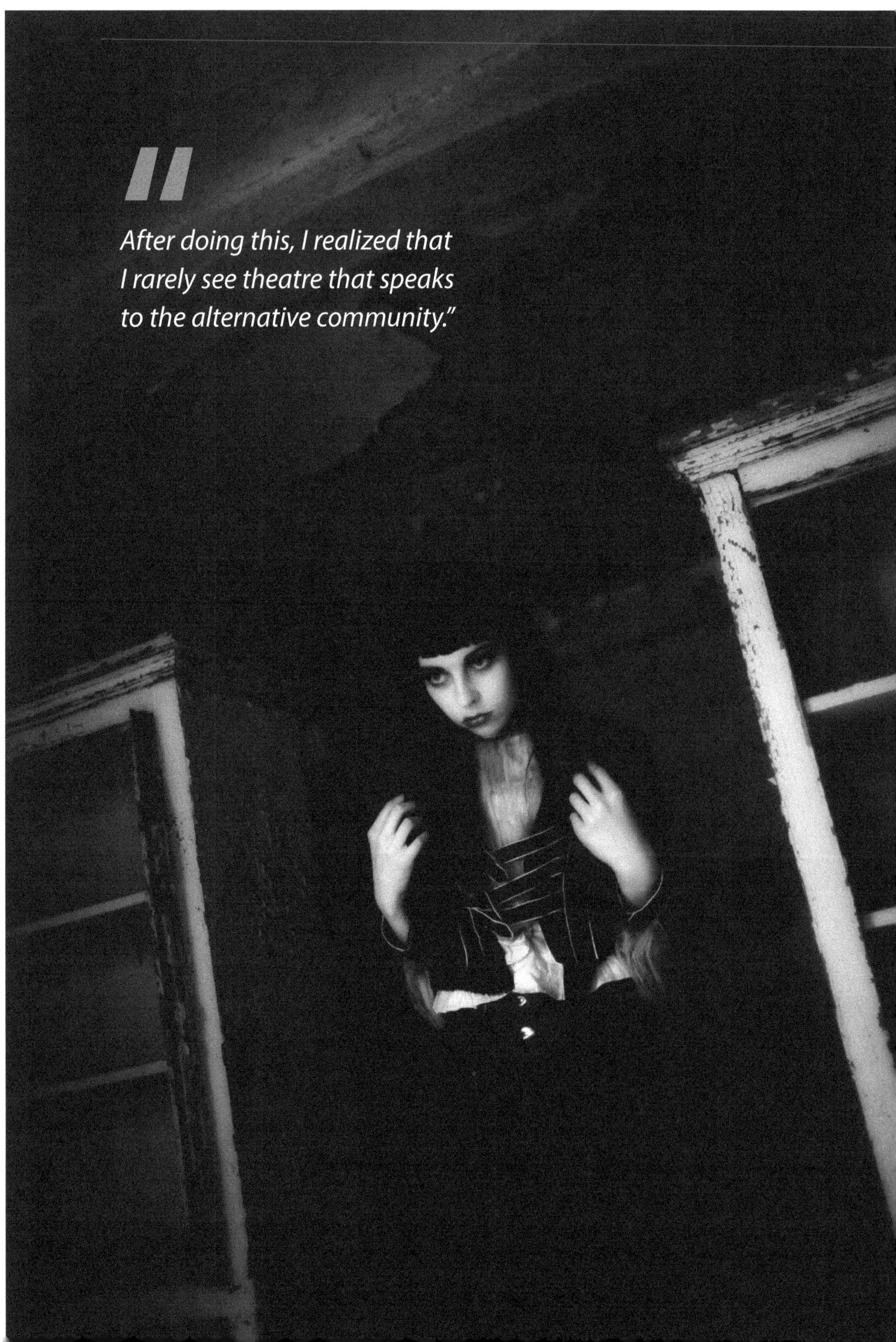
After doing this, I realized that
I rarely see theatre that speaks
to the alternative community."

(Carpe Nocturne) Tell Us About Your Modeling Experience.

(Ophelia Darkly) I've been modeling for a little over two years and I've had the opportunity to work with some extremely talented individuals. I've done fashion modeling, alternative, and art modeling (clothed) with a wonderful artist named Julie Johnson. Some notable photographers I've worked with are: Adamson Studios, renegotiationproof, RedRum Collaboration, and Coma Pill. However, there are so many more photographers I'm dying to work with. Without a car, it's difficult to reach them unfortunately. I like to work with people who have a similar creative aesthetic. When I model, I strive to create something beautiful and poetic. I believe in the power of transformation. Images can really speak so deeply to people. I don't want to just take a "nice photo".

(Carpe Nocturne) Any Other Interesting Info For Our Readers?

(Ophelia Darkly) I created a unique performance piece this past year for my honors thesis project. It incorporated my own dark poetry, my fiancé's dark music (original composition), strange fashion, movement, and wonderful actors. It was all done in two weeks and was called GushHeart. After doing this, I realized that I rarely see theatre that speaks to the alternative community. I am interested in putting together a theatre group that centers around dark themes and explores the mind.

Ophelia Darkly
Chicago, IL
"http://www.modelmayhem.com/769805"

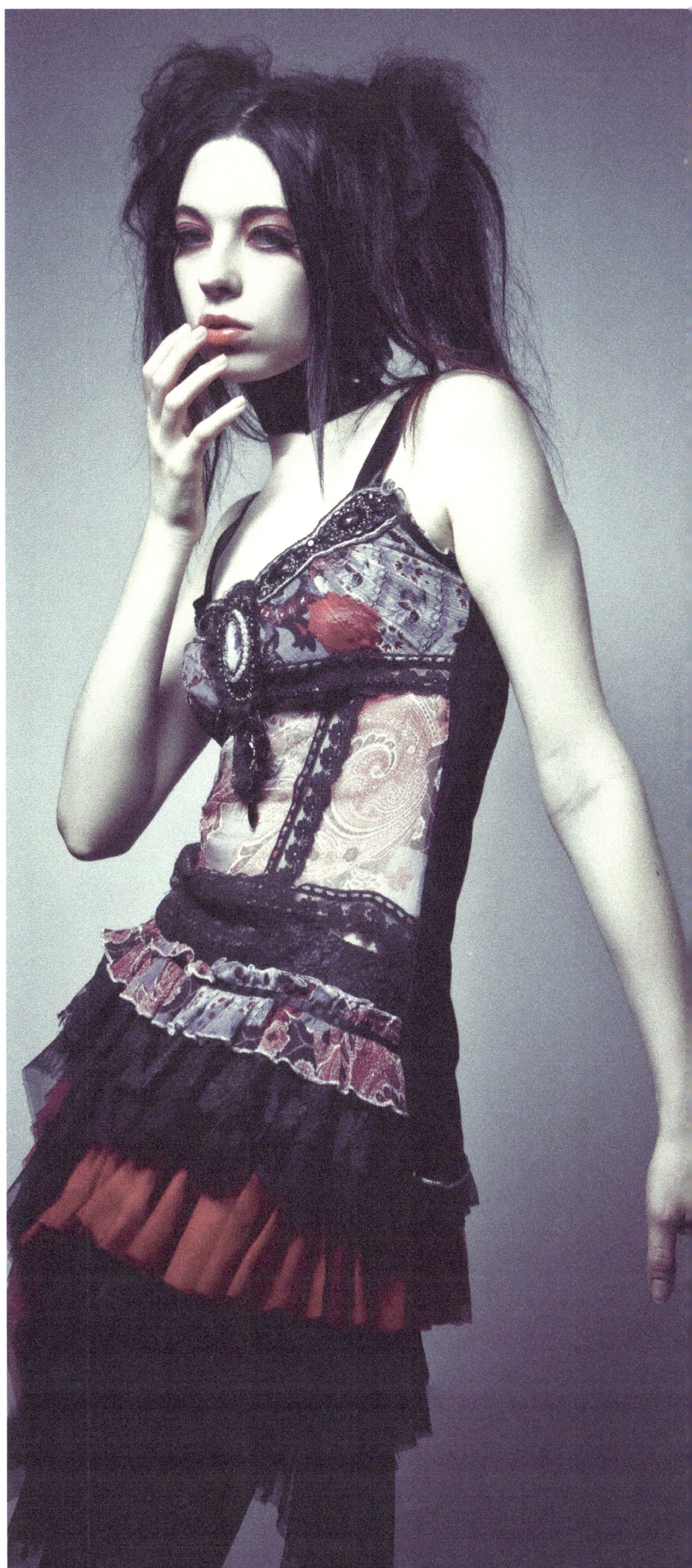

SCARLING

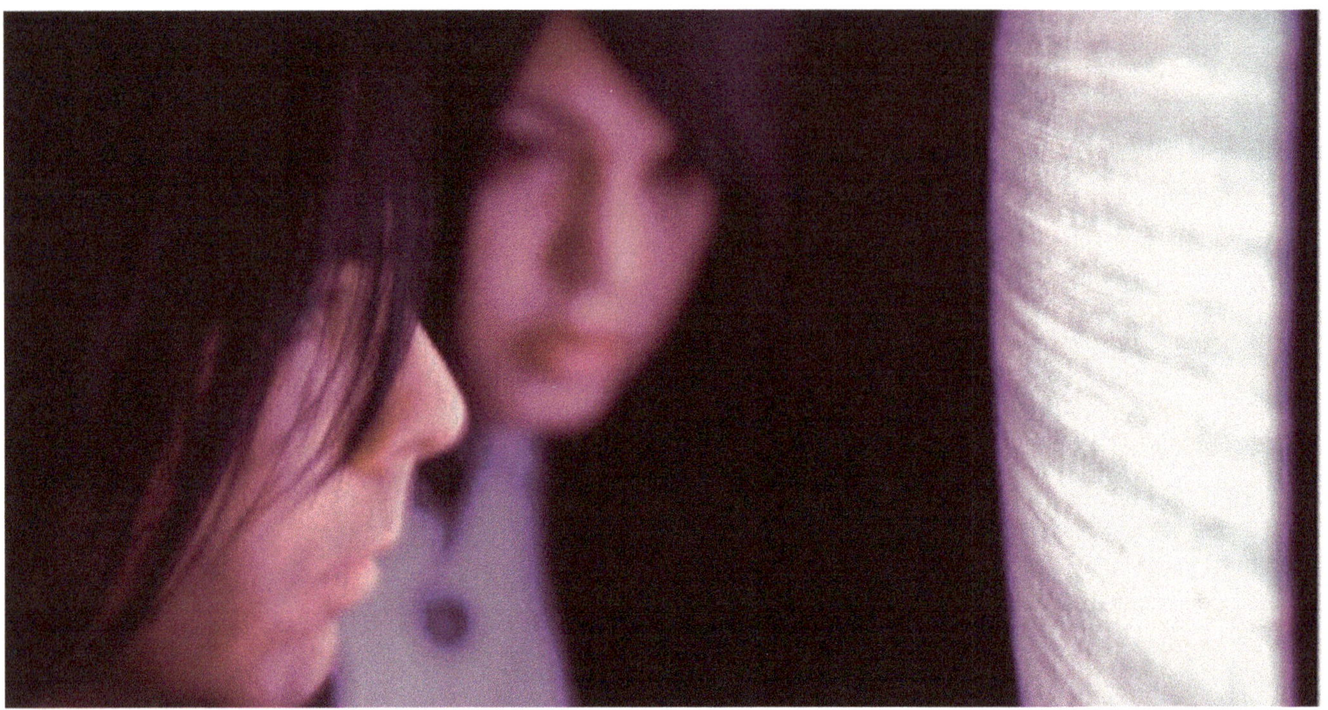

by Michael Jack

Distortion. Noise. Lyrics... sometimes disturbing, always thought provoking. Catchy? Maybe. Noise pop, Shoegaze, I prefer the simpler all-encompassing Goth Rock classification... if I must categorize them. They are Scarling. The band is composed of former Jack Off Jill front woman, Jessicka, and guitarist and visual effects producer, Christian Hejnal. The pair met shortly after the breakup of the aforementioned band, introduced by a mutual friend, and began writing songs together. It was Christian who convinced Jessicka to stay in the music industry. There are many fans who are thankful he did. Two CD's, numerous singles, marriage, and many various visual art projects later...the pair is continuing to wow fans, as we hold our breaths awaiting the soon to be released third full-length CD.

In 2003, Jessicka and Christian released their debut single, "Band Aid Covers the Bullet Hole." The following year saw their first full-length CD released, titled, "Sweet Heart Dealer." The album, as Jessicka related, was inspired by her experimentation with hallucinogenic drugs, and various external sources including the attacks on Sept. 11, 2001 and her band's breakup. The CD was well received, and garnered favorable reviews from such sources as Allmusic, Spin Magazine, and ROCKRGRL, where Jessicka was featured on the cover later that year. Robert Smith of the Cure took notice as well. He invited Scarling to perform on the Curiosa Festival he had organized, and also added them to his Celebrity Playlist on iTunes.

After a series of 7" singles, "So Long, Scarecrow," the band's second full-length album, was released in 2005. The CD was a sharp contrast the their previous work, and nearly double in length. Where "Sweet Heart Dealer," was still reminiscent of that acerbic Jack Off Jill style, "So Long, Scarecrow," was more atmospheric and even more melancholy. Jessicka explained that "Scarecrow" was more of an introspective journey, and attributes much of change in sound to new producer Rob Campanella of The Brian Jonestown Massacre, and to Christian himself. The album was touted as "Resurrecting Goth," by Venus Magazine, and given five out of five stars by Alternative Press. Scarling also began to be compared to such legendary acts as My Bloody Valentine and Sonic Youth.

Since the release of "So Long, Scarecrow," Scarling has taken a long hiatus... from music. The couple has been very busy. Besides being married in 2007, Christian Hejnal has been the visual effects producer for such films as Spider Man 1, 2, and 3, Darkness Falls, Tim Burton's Alice in Wonderland, and Oz the Great and Powerful. Jessicka has turned a lifelong love with visual arts into a successful career. Her paintings and sculptures have been featured in several magazines, displayed throughout the

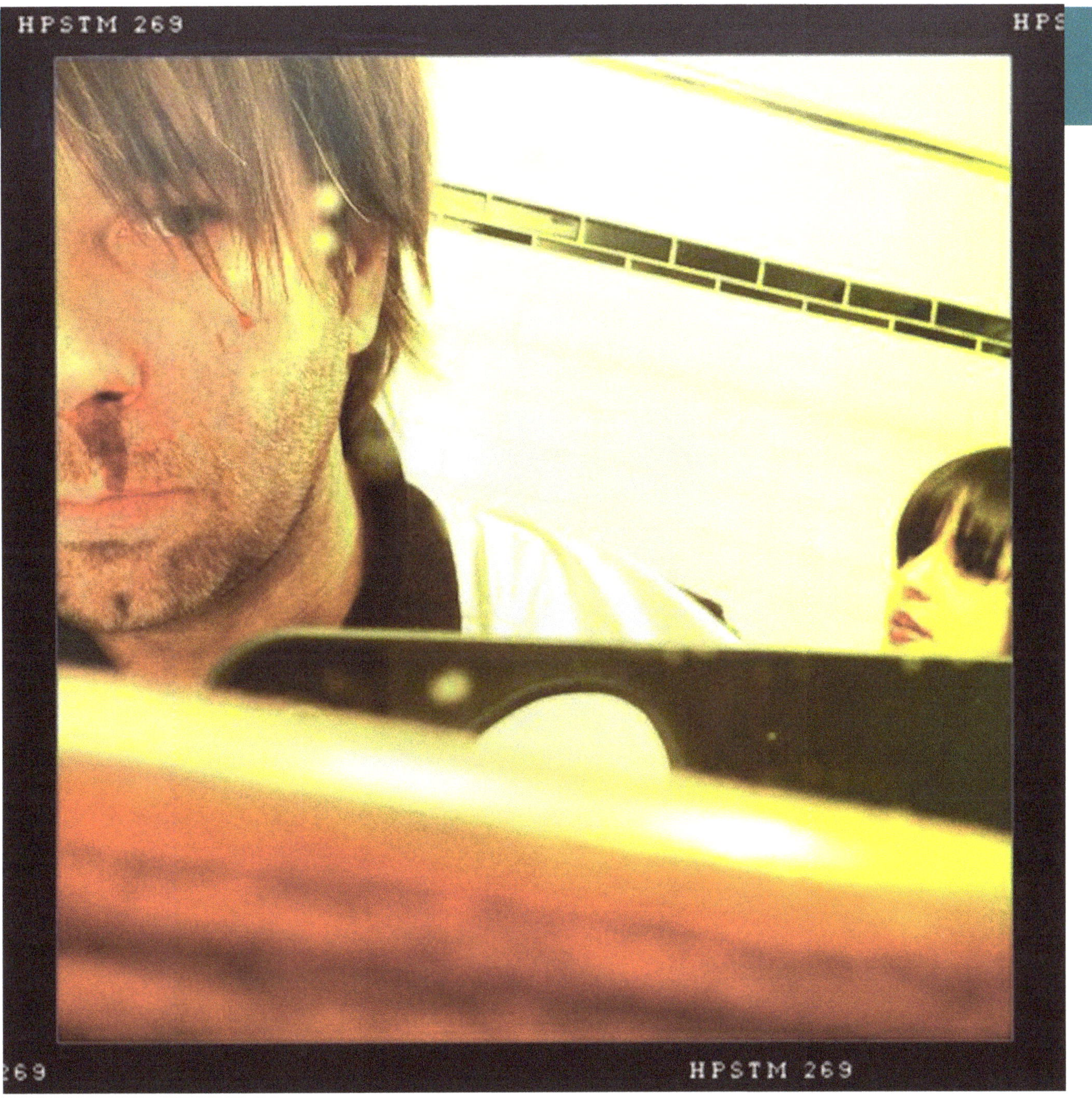

United States, and is the resident curator of Dark Dark Science.

Finally, in 2013, Scarling fans got a taste of what is coming...the long awaited third album. The single "Who Wants to Die for Art?" was released, with B side single "I Started a Joke." The songs fall somewhere in between the first two albums, but my guess is it will be closer to "Scarecrow" with a natural evolution of sound. Time will tell. They definitely did not lose the distortion. Did I mention we are holding our breaths? We wait.

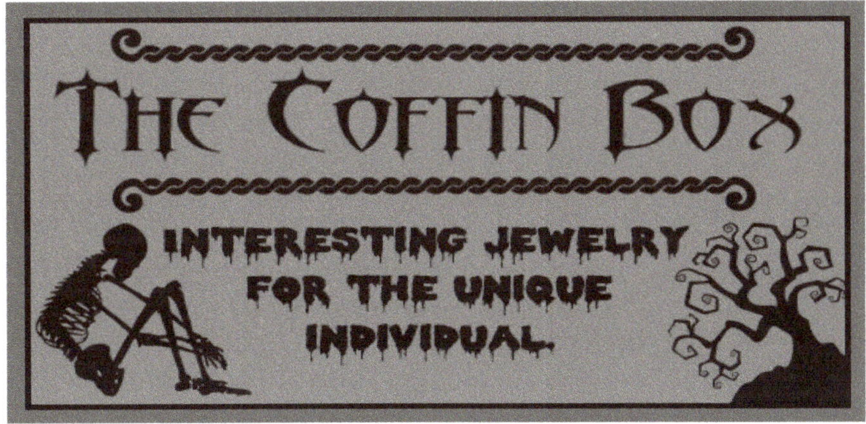

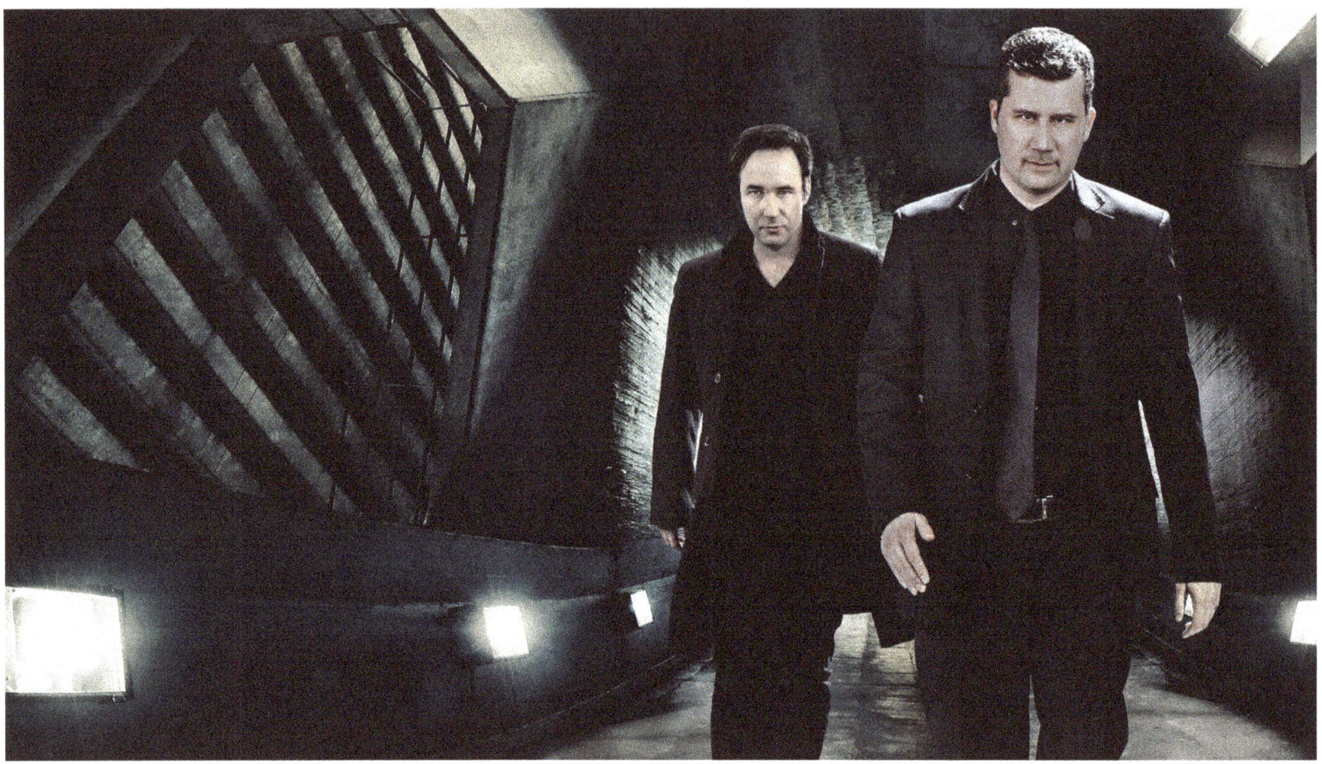

Photo by Jamais Vu & Claudia Schone (Guiding Light)

By Sonnett57

Seabound has always driven their music so it 'reaches out, stimulates your mind and allows you to establish your own personal connection to it. A few of their tracks have even fueled my fire in trying times. Their controversial track 'Exorcise' off of their first release 'No sleep Demon' was what captured my attention and drew me to this band. I loved the track as it had a positive message and a catchy beat. Yet, due to it's the nature of its samples I often caught grief when I spun it at the club and even more when I performed to it. I was living in a very religious city, and my normal everyday working activities were considered a heresy to some. Even though it was just a few words, I looked at playing this track as something that threw religion back in the face of those that had stuffed it in mine. I also have a connection to the very popular track 'Hooked'. The lyrics state the passion, and longing for wanting something that is just out of reach or impossible. I feel it showcases our human nature of how we feel when we would do almost anything to be able to obtain something or be with someone we desire. The feeling of not being able to achieve what I am passionate about is what I consider to be my personal hell.

I was extremely excited when the opportunity to scour the minds of Seabound. It was my chance to ask them about their early years and I had to find out what the band had been up to during their recent hiatus. I was grateful Frank took the time out of his busy schedule and patients for my interview. The role reversal of asking the psychologist the questions was quite fun. Step into my office...

Sonnett57: What projects were each of you in before Seabound?

Frank: Seabound was the first professional project for me. I had toyed with synthesizers, drum-machines and sequencers before, and I had written quite a few songs of my own. However, the whole endeavor gained a strong momentum when Martin and I met. If I am not mistaken, Martin played in a punk band for a while before developing a taste for creating electronic music.

Sonnett57: What inspired you to start creating music?

Frank: I have always been a very musical person. When I was

FACE OF SEABOUND

young, I used to sing for hours on the swing behind my parents' place. Music has also worked very well for me as a refuge. I found comfort and strength in songs. When I discovered the artists and bands that become major influences, like Gary Numan or Front 242, it was always a bit on a revelation to me. Energetic and well-crafted electronic music is among the most powerful forces I have encountered in life. That's why I wanted to become more involved and not only receive and consume, but also create.

Sonnett57: The archives on the website go back to January of 2001. What was going on with Seabound before this?

Frank: Martin and I started working on joint demo material in the mid-90s and put together two full length demos over the years 1995 to 2000. It was then that we were signed to Dependent, and "No Sleep Demon", our first album was released in the year after that.

Photo by Nicole Bringer

Frank: Honestly, I don't recall whether a particular year stands out when it comes to file sharing and Seabound. I believe that for all bands, it has been a continuous process, and the present independent music world is hardly comparable to the situation 10 years ago. We all have to accept that. Plus, we are part of the phenomenon. It is true that our first demo was leaked a couple of years ago, and we were not so happy about that. Other than that, we are affected just like everybody else, I guess. A couple of bands have fully embraced the new digital age. The Legendary Pink Dots, for example, are expanding their vast back catalogue online tirelessly. It's almost impossible to keep track. Other bands appear to have a more difficult time to adapt. I personally miss the physical products and being inspired by physical products (be it vinyl or cd) in a good record store. But I can also see the benefits. The 12,000 cds I have collected over the years weigh two tons if you add in the storage racks. That can become a real burden if you decide to ever move (laughs).

Sonnett57: It appears that your first major release went straight to the DAC, What were your feelings about this? Were you prepared to for instant success?

Frank: We were very grateful, of course. Our first single was called "Travelling" and it was co-produced by Covenant's Eskil Simonsson. We worked on that track with him in a Berlin home and realized in the process that our material had potential to appeal to clubs. At the same time we never wanted to become a club act because Seabound songs always aim at different levels, not just the feet (laughs).

Sonnett57: In seems in 2004 you have had a few problems with illegal downloading and piracy. Do you believe that file sharing sources like Bandcamp and ITunes have helped the music industry?

Sonnett57: What was happening with Seabound during the hiatus from 2009- 2011?

Frank: Martin left Germany to live and work in the US. He married and became and entertainment lawyer on the west coast. It took quite some time for him to settle in and sort out the many business and life-related issues. Plus, shipping his studio turned out to be an adventure in itself. I stayed busy working with my side-projects Edge of Dawn and Ghost & Writer and I strongly believe that this contributed to the grown maturity you hear in this Seabound's album "Speak in Storms", released earlier this year.

Sonnett57: Your website archives play out a thorough history of the band through the years—almost like a journal. Do you

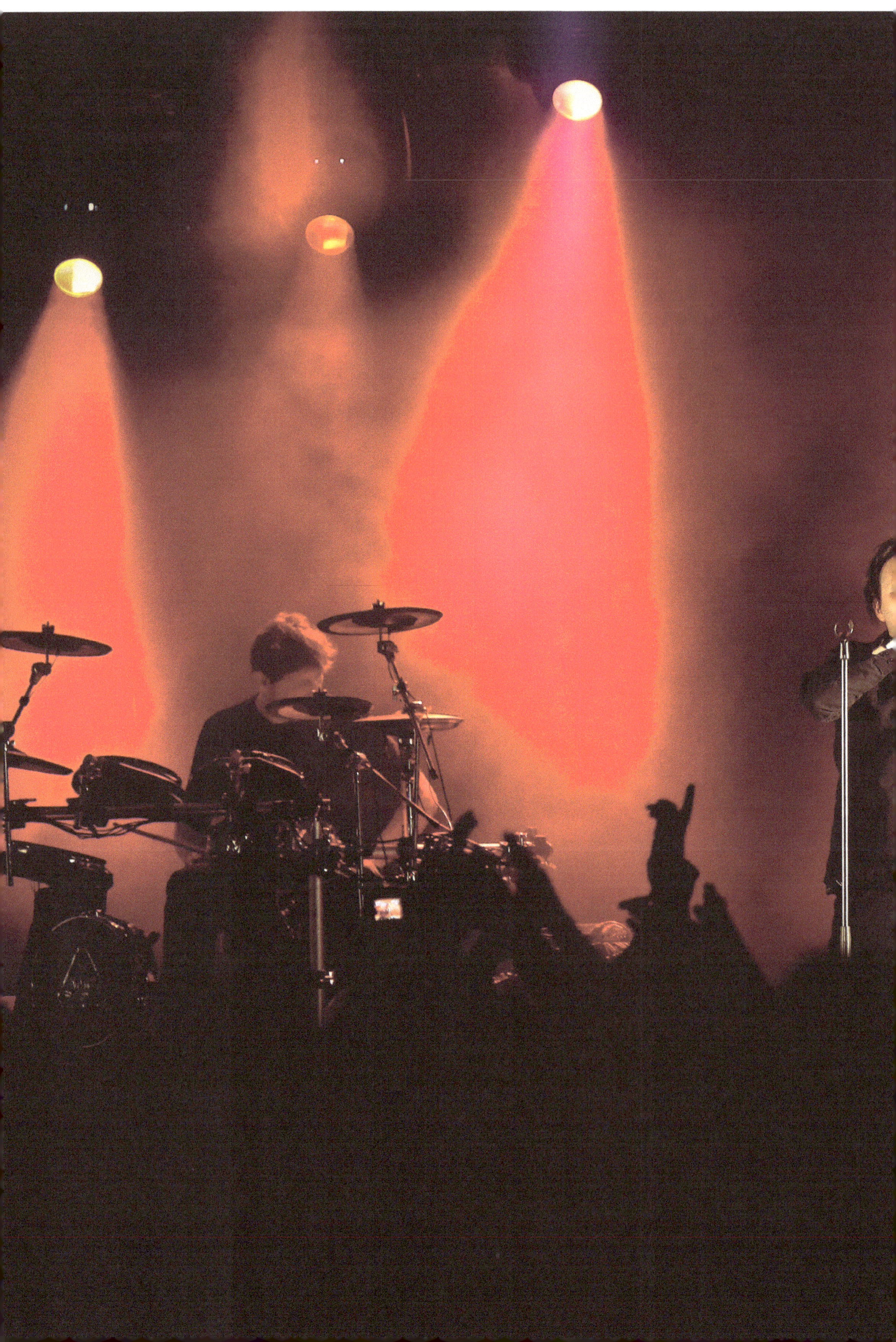

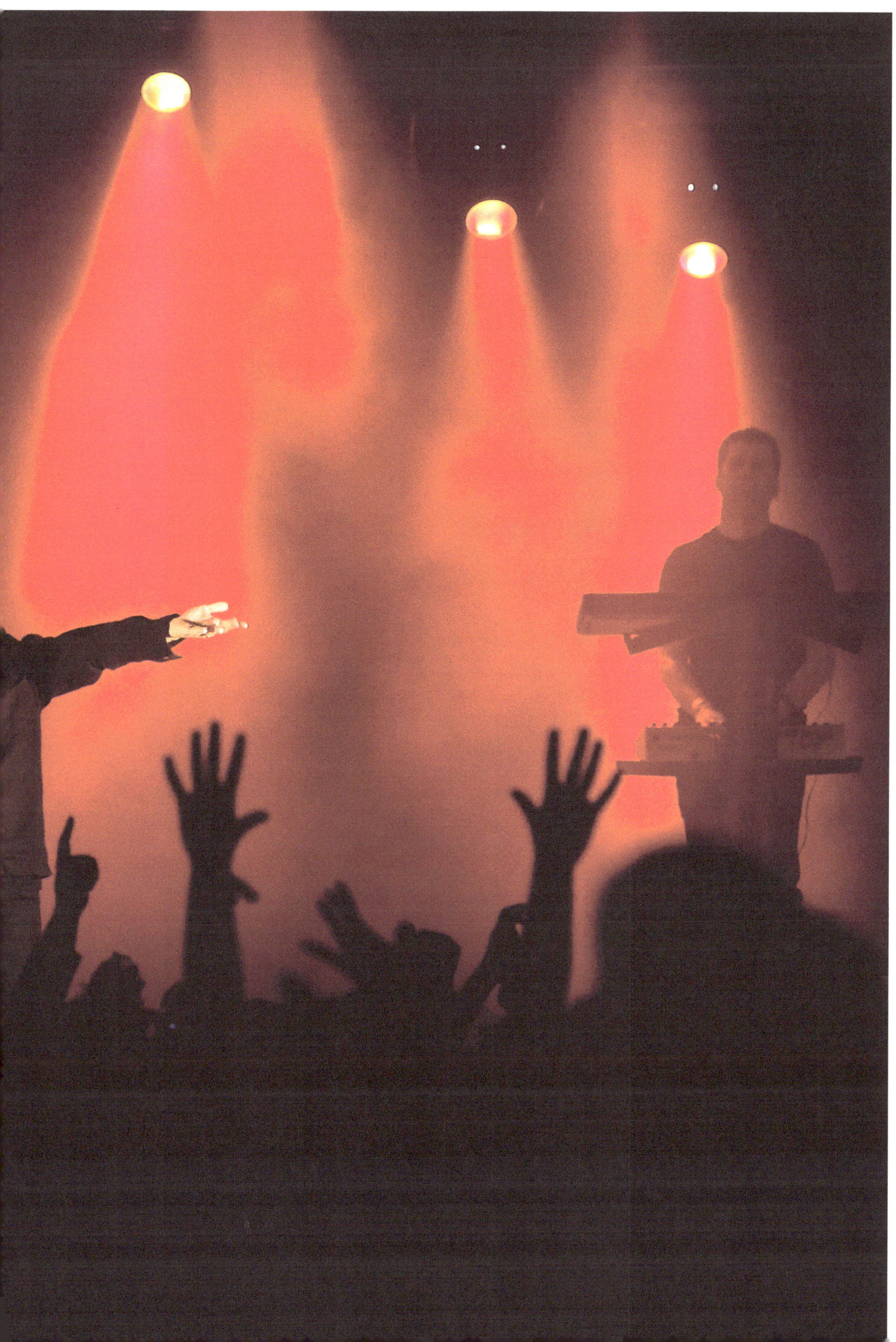

reflect back on it at all and wish there were things you had done differently and does it inspire new ideas?

Frank: I honestly don't. In my personal life I increasingly have the impression that time flies in an almost obscene way. The moments when I am free from work or family duties, I'd rather enjoy myself instead of moaning about the what if's of the past.

Sonnett57: What side projects do each of you currently have?

Frank: I am working on new material with Mario from Edge of Dawn at the moment and there's Radioaktivists, a musical conspiracy consisting of Daniel Myer (Haujobb, Architect), Krischan Wesenberg (Rotersand), Sascha Lange and myself. We plan to release an album next year and will perform live in January 2015 at the infamous Planet Myer Day in Leipzig, Germany. There's a teaser track on the 2012 Dependence release called "Pieces of Me" which was very well-received, I hear. Ghost & Writer took a break but I wouldn't rule out the possibility of resurrection sometime in the future.

Sonnett57: Can we expect a Speak In Storms tour here in the US?

Frank: Absolutely! We love to play in the US, and we have plans to tour in March-April 2015. As soon as we have reliable information, we will share it with you and our American friends.

Sonnett57: What is on the horizon for Seabound?

Frank: The US tour would be the next big item on the menu for us. And, of course, write new songs. Fortunately, we are under no pressure whatsoever when it comes to the creative process. It shouldn't take another 7 years before the next Seabound release though.

Sonnett57: When not working on music, what occupies your time?

Frank: I am a psychologist with a focus on research which is a time-consuming business since I am involved in a number of research projects. And of course, there's the teaching, too. I also have two young children who I love to spend my time with.

Sonnett57: Most artist get inspiration from life experiences for their songs. Does Frank get inspiration from the knowledge he gained while getting his psychology degree as well?

Frank: Yes, my interest in why individuals become who they are and do what they do is the driving force behind both my research and my writing. The writing has the additional benefit that I can make up things and stage stories to my liking. That's something scientists shouldn't do (laughs).

Sonnett57: Who does the majority of the writing?

Frank: In Seabound we have developed a clear division of labor over the years: Martin creates instrumental songs and structures, I write the lyrics and record the vocals. Of we mutually like what we hear, we turn to the fine-tuning. A song that sounds complete to the outsider may still undergo change and is tweaked until both Martin and I are fully satisfied. Working this way has proven effective for us because we rarely pull the plug on a track at the last minute. Also, there's no vast archive of unreleased material this way.

Sonnett57: What is the ideal venue for you to play in?

Frank: I love to play in clubs that have a certain atmosphere and history. Places like the "Whiskey A GoGo" in L.A. where The Doors had also played or the "Kaiserkeller" in Hamburg where the Beatles played in their very early days have that. In general, I like to be able to make contact with the audience, so I enjoy stages that have medium size elevation only, if that makes sense.
Be sure to check out and pick up their newest release "Speak In Storms". Frank feels it is their best work yet and I concur.

Previous Page: Photo by Claudia Schone

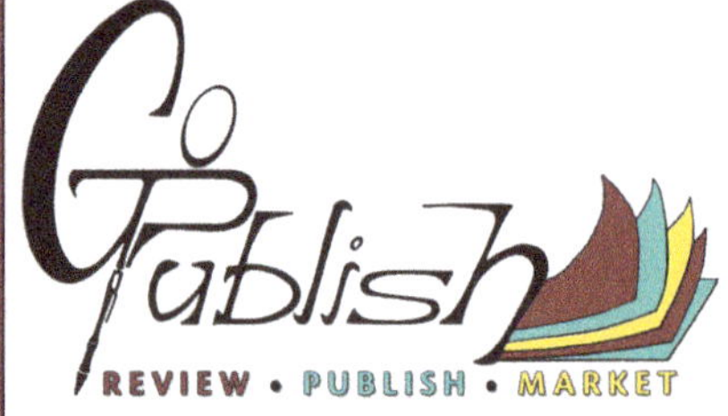

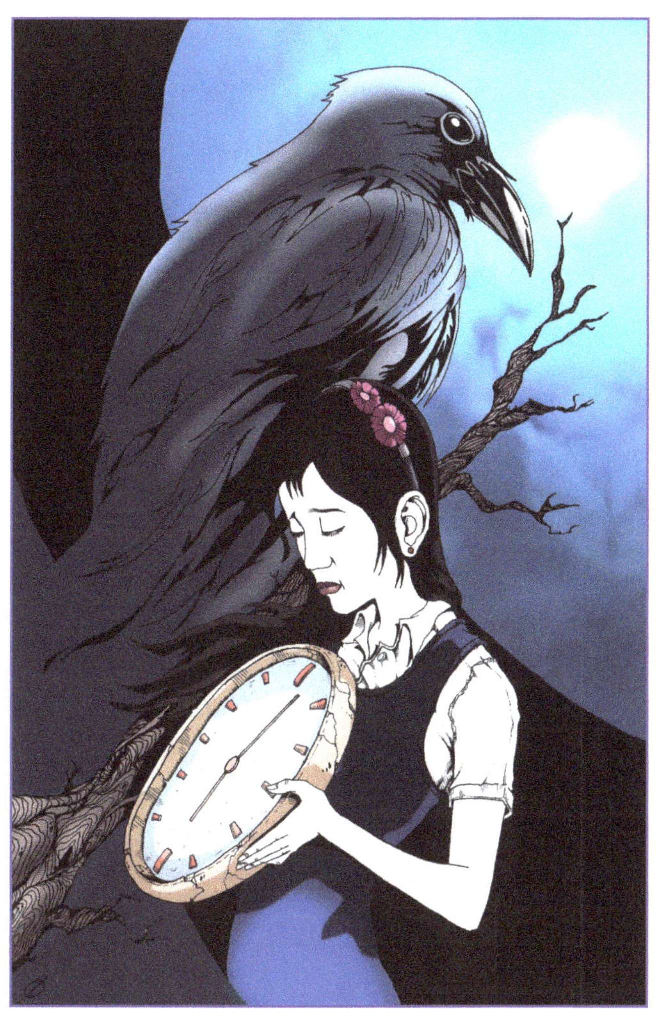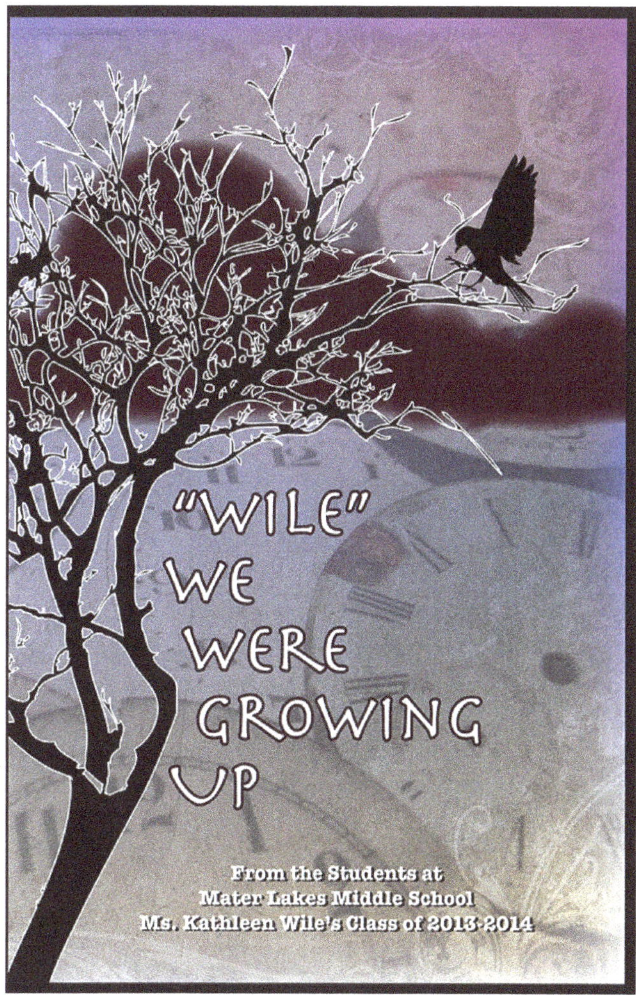

Featured in the Miami Herald

**"Wile" We Were Growing Up:
From The Students At Mater Lakes Middle School,
Ms. Kathleen Wile's Class of 2013 – 2014**

Ms. Wile does everything possible to make the learning process enjoyable
and life changing for her students.

Read stories from Mater Lakes Class of 2013 – 2014: Alexandra Menendez, Camila Del Sol, Dymilly Rivera, Gabriella Montero, Isabella Gonzalez, Jacqueline Canut, Jaynah Geneus, Karla Flores, Mariana M. Pirri, Michael Buitrago, Monica Sanchez, Natalie Perez, Samantha Castro, Seleste Arauz, Sianna Rivera, Sophia Leonetti, Tatiana Llerena, Vanessa Ramos

On sale. BUY YOUR COPY NOW
at www.visualadjectives.com

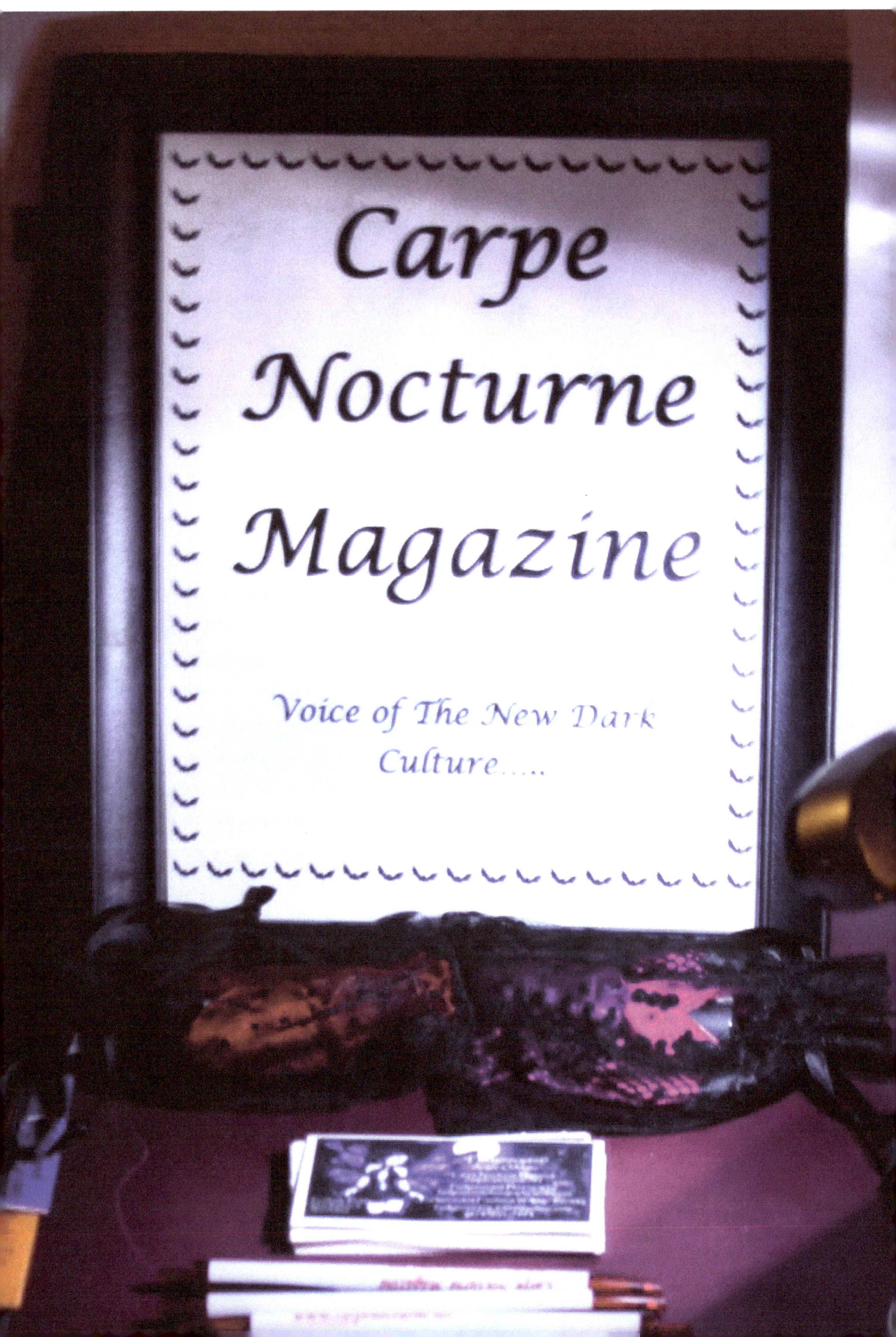

Carpe
Nocturne
Magazine

Voice of The New Dark
Culture.....

OUT AND ABOUT
NEW ORLEANS

by Fairlyinnocent

Southern Gothic Festival (SoGo) is an annual gothic gathering in New Orleans that started in 2010 with founders Lesleigh Frankenstein (DJ Vendetta) and Valek Reed. Southern Gothic Festival occurred July 10 through July 13. Every new year brings a new name and this year's SoGo was called Southern Gothic Festival Year 5: Ascension. For this SoGo, founder Valek Reed collaborated with his wife Dee Anachka as well as Carolyn Luscomb and Sara Ico who got involved due to the love of the scene. The group collaborating brought a WONDERFUL new take on Southern Gothic festival. Valek and Dee took on the art exhibits Thursday as well as an additional showing on Saturday afternoon, and Sunday's SoGo closing festivities. Carolyn Luscomb and Sara Ico were responsible for the bands and DJ's Friday and Saturday in addition to the tours that were set up on Saturday and Sunday.

Thursday, day one; the event started with an art show exhibited at a location called St. Joe Lofts, which is subsidized housing for artists and also used as an event venue. There was a champagne toast to start the first art exhibit as well as Valek and Dee's official New Orleans wedding. There was a bar available for libations as well as Whors d'oeuvres to satiate the patrons. The artists were on site to discuss their displayed pieces of work. As the night progressed some open mic performances were shared. Kurt Amacker, a writer and lead organizer of Fangtasia Vampire Ball, read from his graphic novel. Next up was Valek Reed, from S.O.L.O., followed by Eric Fellows of Lovacaine, both of whom gave acoustic performances. To continue the party there was a DJ showcase night at the Wolf's Den. DJs spinning this night were DJ Ruinr out of Colorado Springs, CO, DJs Neea Starla and Samari from Pittsburg, PA. The art was available for purchase on site and can also be purchased on each artist's websites.

Friday night was held at the Wolf's Den with bands and vendors from the art show. This year's MC was Lord Chaz, best known as one of the creators of the French Quarter ghost and vampire tours. He is an actor, author, and musician and did an amazing job keeping things moving during the SoGo events. DJ Seraph out of Atlanta, GA was spinning first on this night, and in between band sets, until S.O.L.O. took the stage. This is a band and project of Valek Reed, one of the original founders of Southern Gothic Festival. He played to the audience with dark industrial overtones getting the night started with a bang along with boundless beats for the goths to move about to. Next was Lovacaine kicking it up on stage with their amazing vocals and guitar riffs also bringing dancers to their feet, working up a sweat, to the fantastic music they were listening to. A surprise burlesque performance by dancer Lady Lucerne was amazing with an illusory shedding of one's skin revealing an inner beauty as one of her sets. She was a wonderful addition to the night's performers and amidst her performing a band called The Greatest Fear took the stage. This female lead had an astounding multi range voice that belted out tunes smooth as butter! She had this sweet smile and face and you can't believe this is the same person on stage with these powerful vocals coming from within her. When she started singing it seemed to make all the goths in the club sit up and take notice.

The Southern Gothic Festival in New Orleans a yearly event proudly sponsored by Carpe Nocturne.

Photos by Fairlyinnocent

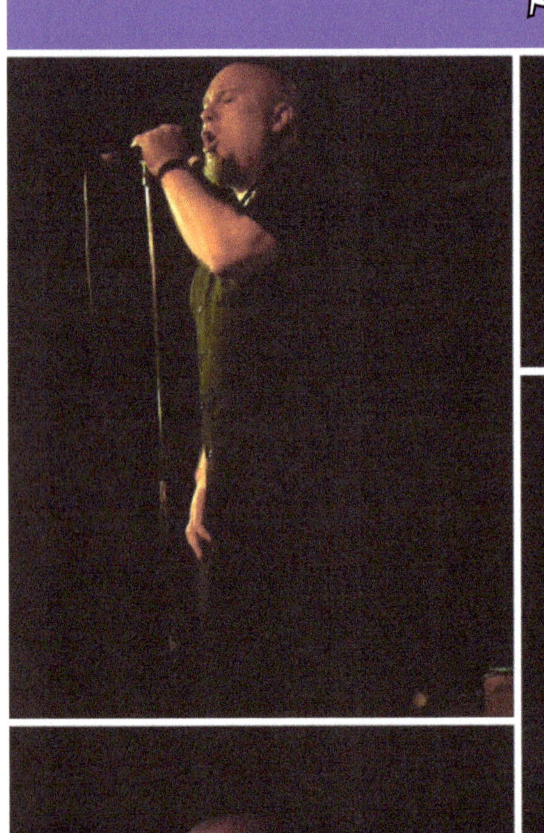

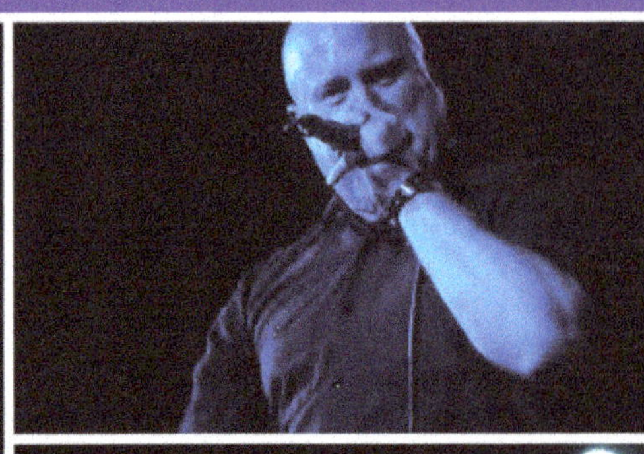

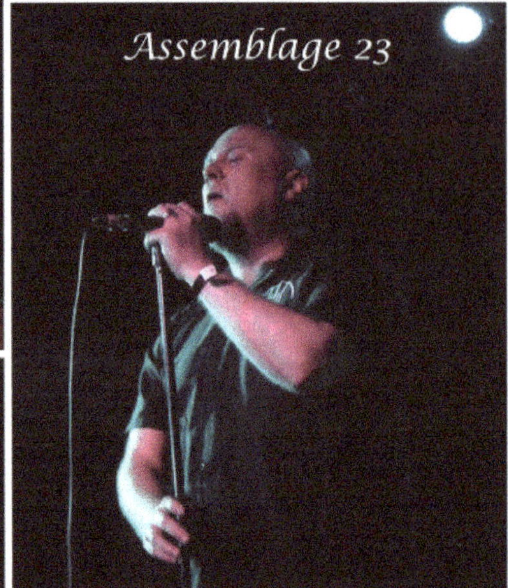

Assemblage 23

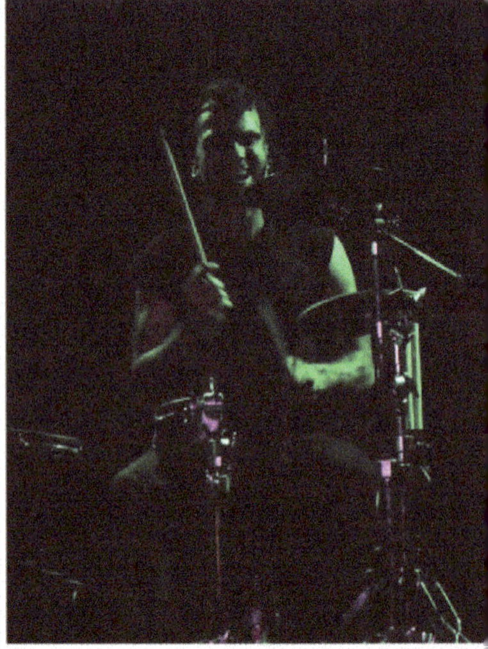

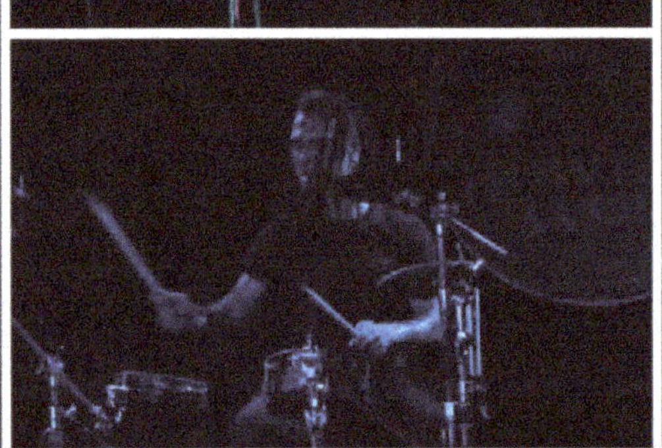

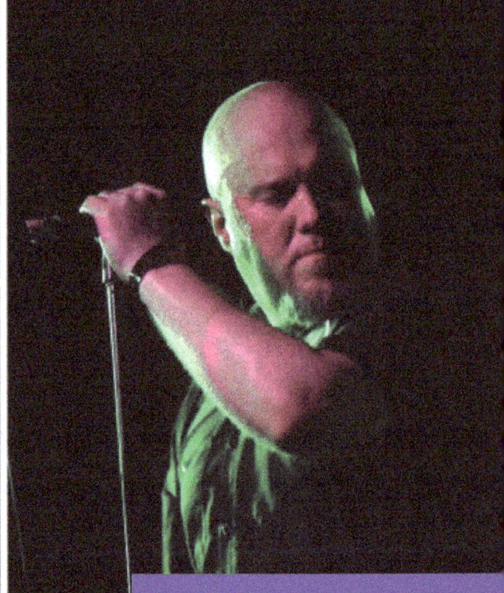

Assemblage 23

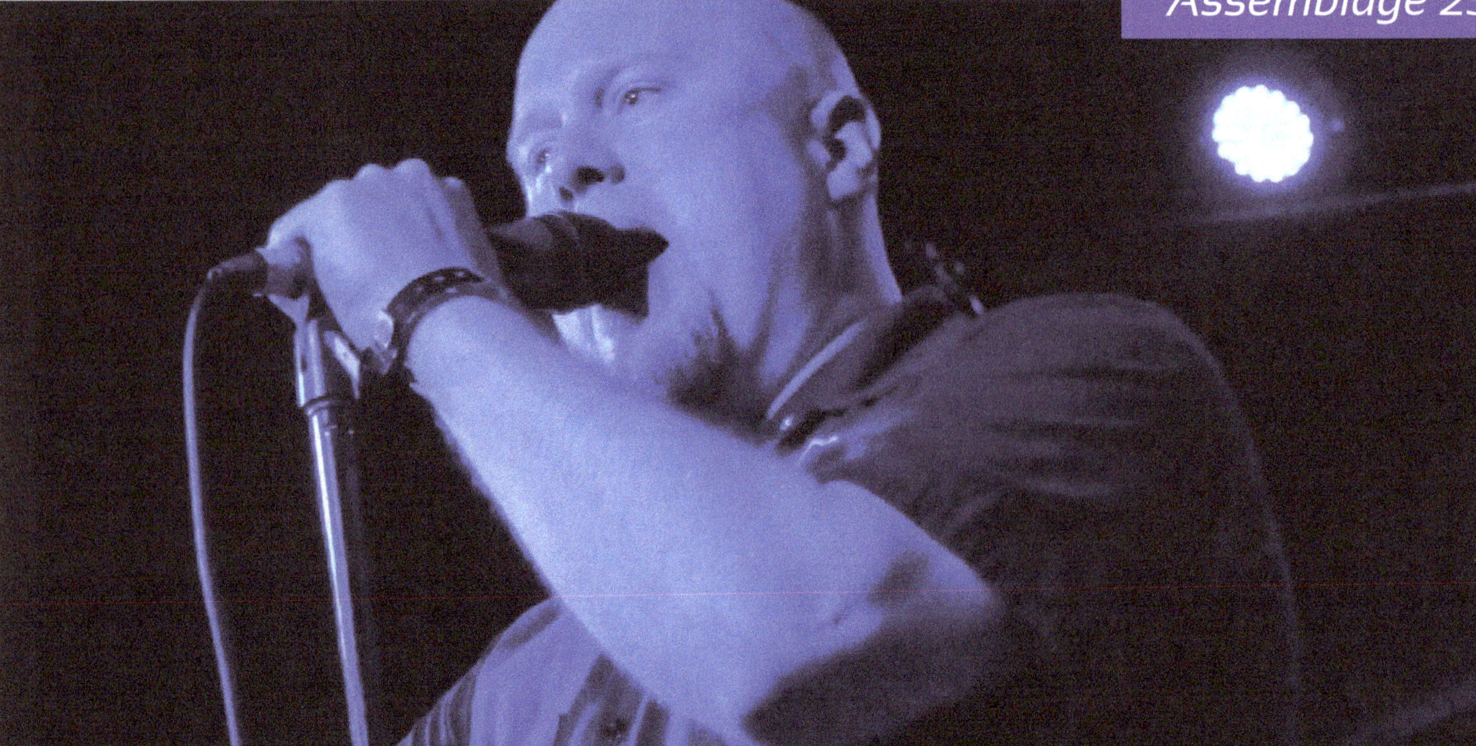

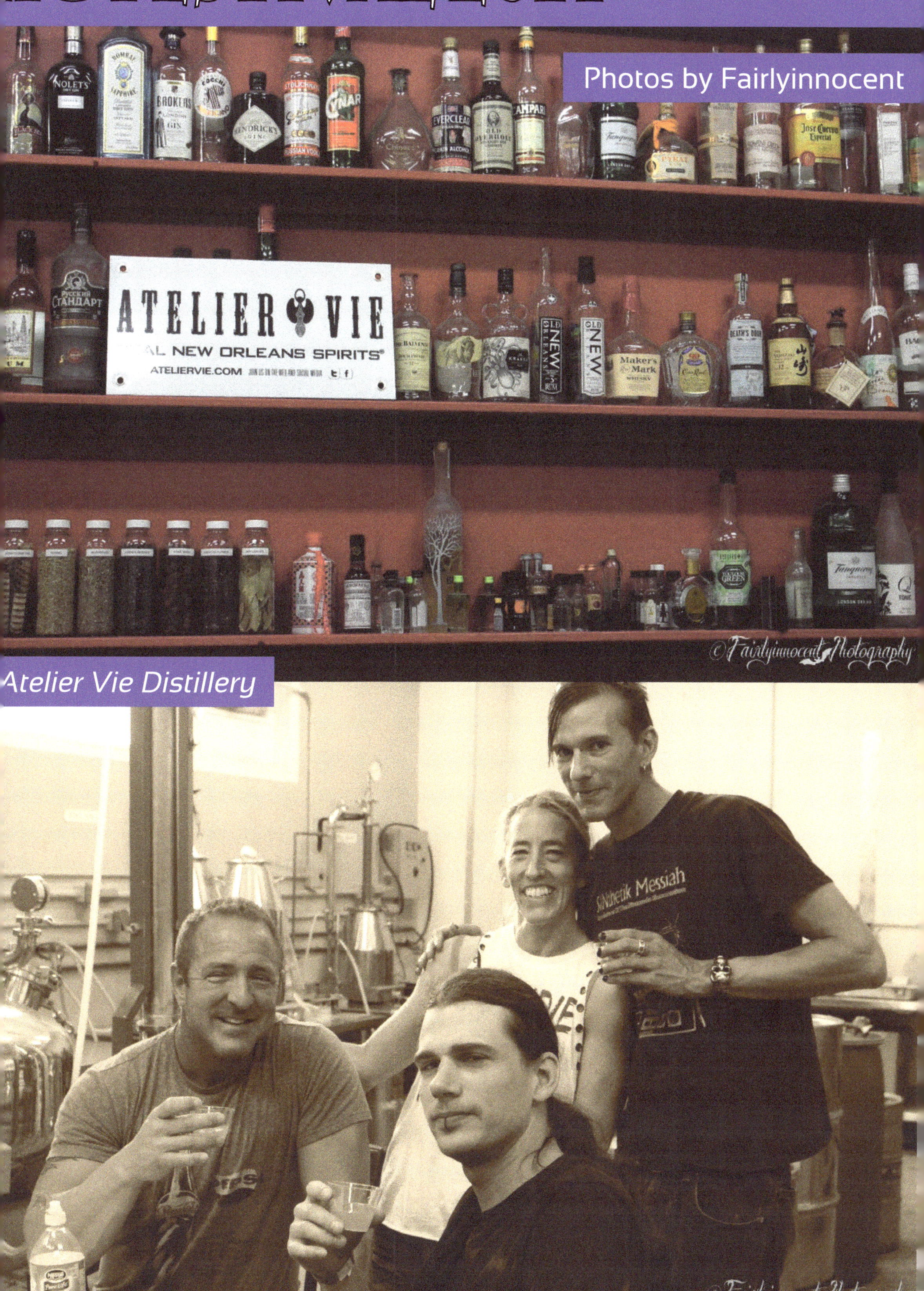

IC FESTIVAL 2014
Photos by Fairlyinnocent
Atelier Vie Distillery
©Fairlyinnocent Photography

This band rocked the house-what a way to close out the bands for Friday night. The rest of the evening was DJ's on the decks spinning a great mix of EBM, Goth, and any dark wave sounds in between by DJ Lore, who is known for his master fangsmith capabilities, and was in house creating fangs for the crowds, and DJ Tom Shear, of the astounding, unparalleled Assemblage 23. This was an impressive second night.

On Saturday, the third day, there were tours set up to a distillery called Atelier Vie. This is a relatively new distillery with a great quality of liquor. We got to see the process of making the various liquors as well as participated in a tasting. We also received a t-shirt as part of our tour. The owners are very knowledgeable and friendly so if you get a chance, stop by the distillery and say you heard about the through The Southern Gothic Festival or SoGo Carpe Nocturne Magazine article.

Saturday night opens with DJ's Ruinr & Neea Starla spinning in The Wolf's Den. Vendors are still available to purchase their wares as well as band merch. The night is starting off a bit more crowded and seems to have a lot more goths in the club. People are buzzing outside and excitement is building as this is the first time that Assemblage 23 has ever played the Southern Gothic Festival. They are the headlining band this year and there are a lot of folks who are ecstatic about seeing Assemblage 23 (Tom Shear) live. First band up is Standard Issue Citizen with some really banging hard industrial beats. Their all-encompassing brand is getting people up early to the floor and letting loose getting the night started early. Up next is Infekt with a metal sounding influence and ass kicking guitars that are melodious and raucous all at the same time. The music penetrates deep into the thought processes but definitely danceable and pleasurable to listen to. Last up is headliner Assemblage 23 with the audience well pumped, sweating from all the dancing to the two previous incredible bands. The Wolf's Den is full of goths with anticipation of a musician who has touched every aspect of their lives at some point with Tom Shear's expressive, touching, and passionate songs with lyrics that incite so many emotions and feelings of love, hurt, and angst. The list is endless and so is the amount of devotion these fans have. Looking around the club you can see how his music affects them. One of the biggest highlights of the weekend was to see this performance and the appreciation the SoGo crowd had. DJ Seraph of Atlanta, GA and DJ Lost Twisted Soul out of New Orleans, LA was on deck to close out the night and send the gothlings home until the Sunday festivities begin.

Sunday was the farewell pool party at the St. Vincent's Guesthouse, which was the host hotel again this year. Carpe Nocturne was not there for the final pool party but was very low key according to Dee Anachka and stated that guests from New Zealand came and set off a spectacular display of fireworks over the pool. DJ Nihil was spinning music until about 3 am and she also stated that this year's party came complete with the standard dose of drunken debauchery keeping SoGo the favorite gathering of goths. There was a ghost tour set up with Lord Chaz Sunday night for those who wanted to partake in this activity. Overall this was an extraordinary four days of art, tours, music, and partying. Will you be at Southern Gothic Festival next year? Keep up to date on everything SoGo at https://www.facebook.com/SoGoFest. From Carpe Nocturne Magazine, a big thank you goes out to everyone who was involved in this year's Southern Gothic Festival.

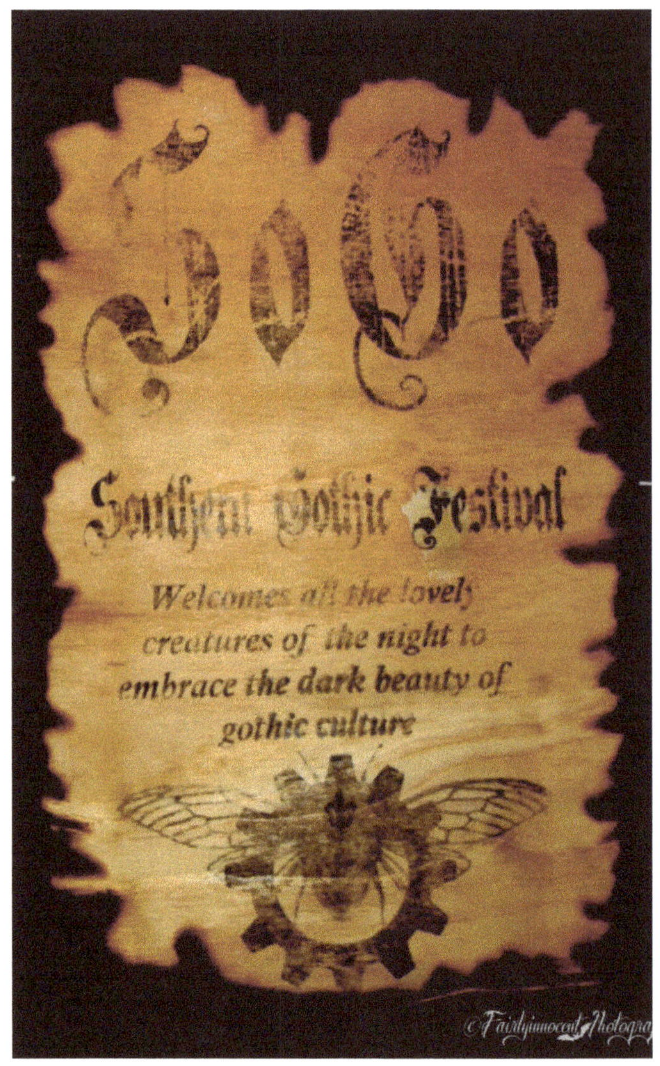

ARTISTS AND OPEN MIC PERFORMERS
Kristof Corvinus: https://www.facebook.com/TheBlackTulipStudio
John and Elizabeth Kuhn: https://www.facebook.com/darqarts
John Allen: https://www.facebook.com/DarkandTwistyArtwork
Josie Buras: https://www.facebook.com/Mygothicfairytales
Chris Prik: https://www.facebook.com/Prikart
Valek Reed: https://www.facebook.com/valek.reed
Valek Reed (Acoustic Performance):   https://www.facebook.com/pages/SOLO/536196013164225
Kurt Amacker: https://www.facebook.com/KurtAmackerComics
Eric Fellows (Acoustic Performance): https://www.facebook.com/lovacainemusic

TOURS
Atelier Vie Distillery: www.ateliervie.com
Lord Chaz Tours: http://www.lordchaz.com

DJ'S
DJ Ruinr - Colorado Springs, CO: https://www.facebook.com/DjRuinr
DJ Neea Starla - Colorado Springs, CO: https://www.facebook.com/DjNeeaStarla
DJ Samarai - Pittsburgh, PA: https://www.facebook.com/pages/DJ-Samarai/1430153477230730
DJ Nihil - Albuquerque, NM: https://www.facebook.com/NihiloserProductions
DJ Seraph - Atlanta, GA: https://www.facebook.com/archangelseraph
DJ Lost Twisted Soul - New Orleans, LA: https://facebook.com/beau.brouillette1
DJ (Maven) Lore - New Orleans, LA: https://www.facebook.com/djfangpimp

ST. VINCENT'S GUESTHOUSE: **http://www.stvguesthouse.com/**
THE HOWLIN WOLF / WOLF'S DEN: **http://www.thehowlinwolf.com**
ST. JOE LOFT'S: **https://www.facebook.com/stjoelofts**

BURLESQUE DANCER
Lady Lucerne: Thelady Lucerne

FANGSMITH
Maven Lore: http://www.darkawakenings.com

BANDS
S.O.L.O. - https://www.facebook.com/pages/SOLO/536196013164225
Lovacaine - https://www.facebook.com/lovacainemusic
The Greatest Fear – http://www.thegreatestfear.com
Standard Issue Citizen – https://www.facebook.com/StandardIssueCitizen
Infekt – http://weareinfekt.com
Assemblage 23 – http://www.assemblage23.com

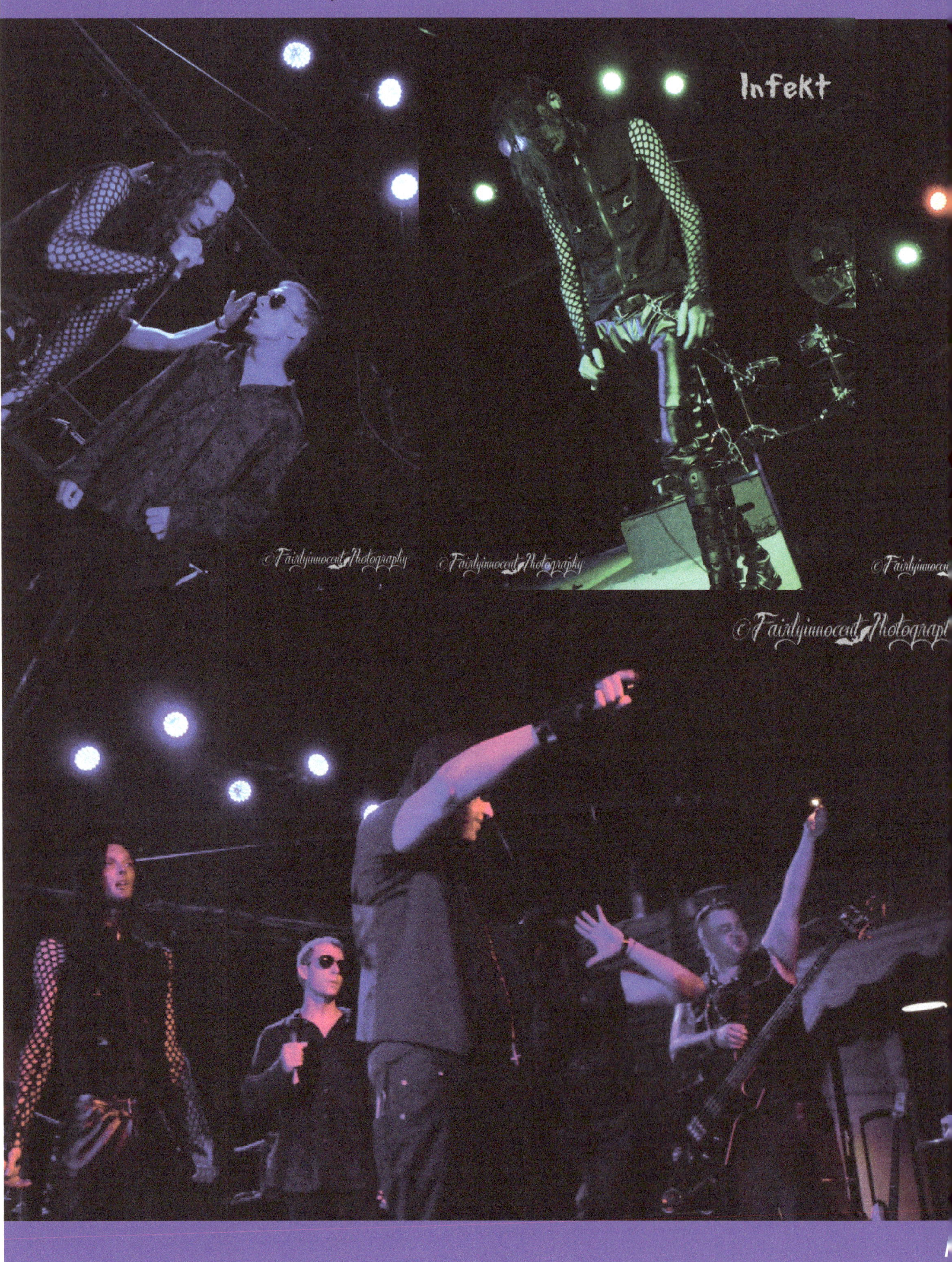
Infekt

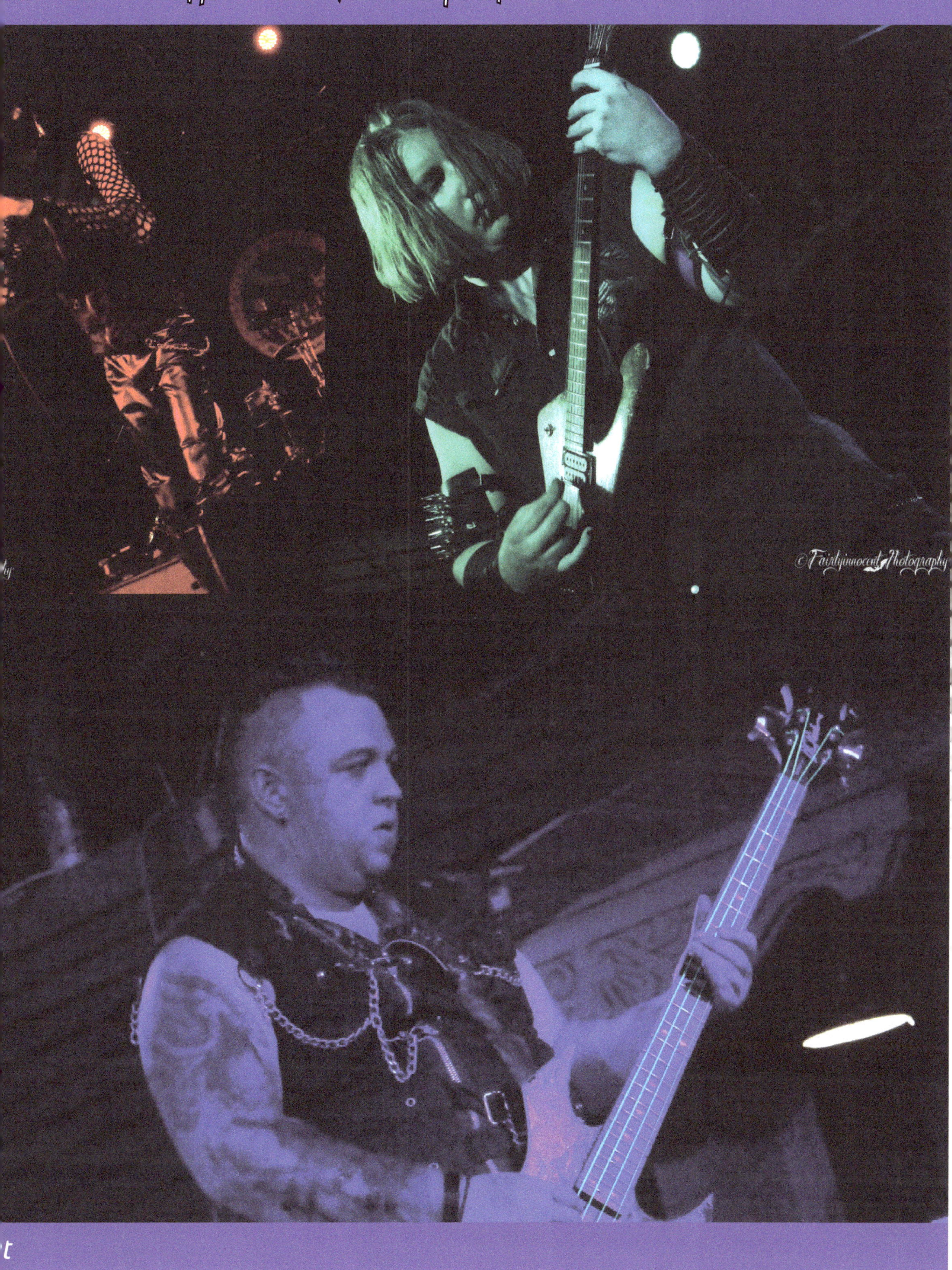

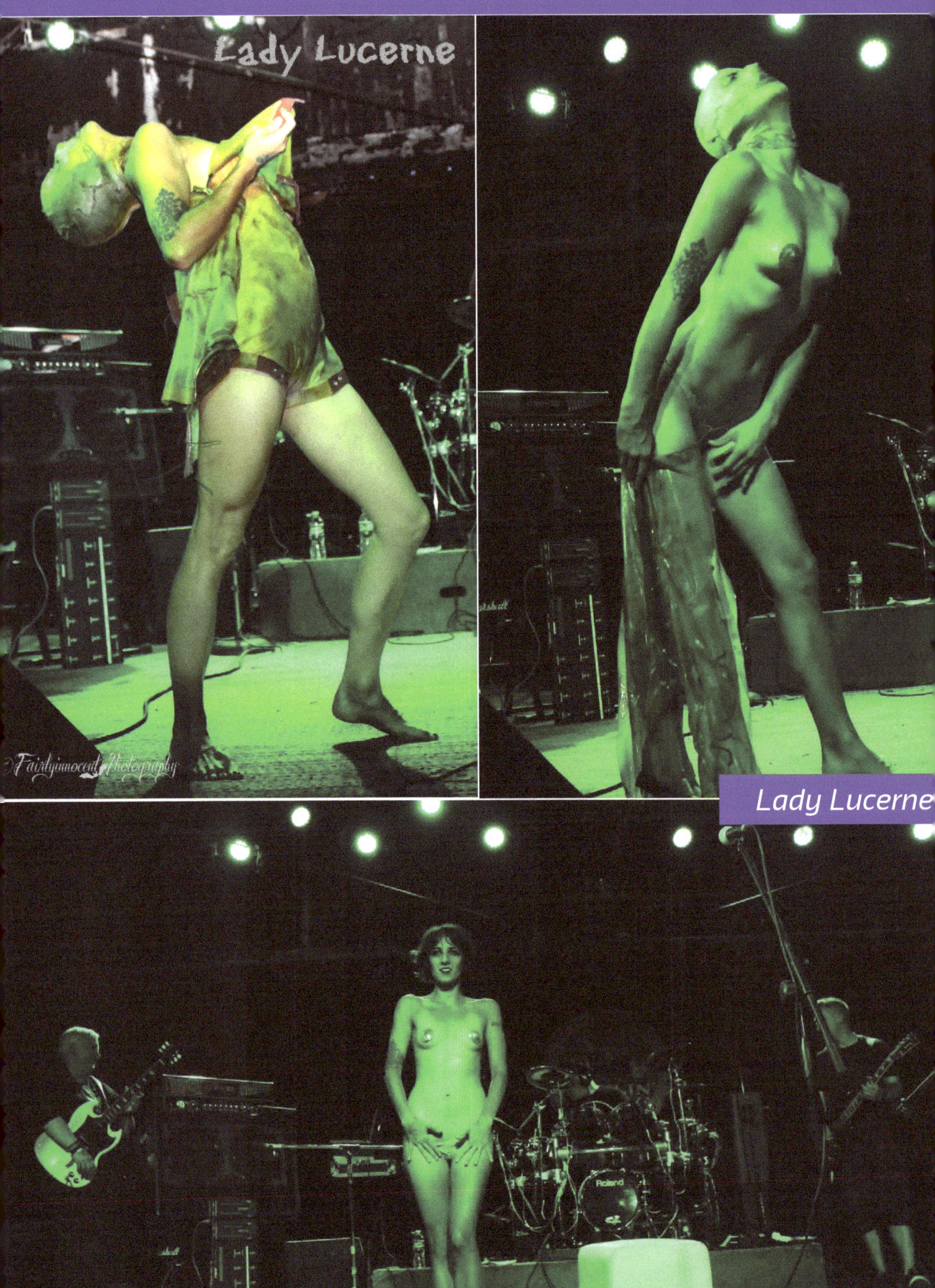
Lady Lucerne
Fairlyinnocent Photography
Lady Lucerne

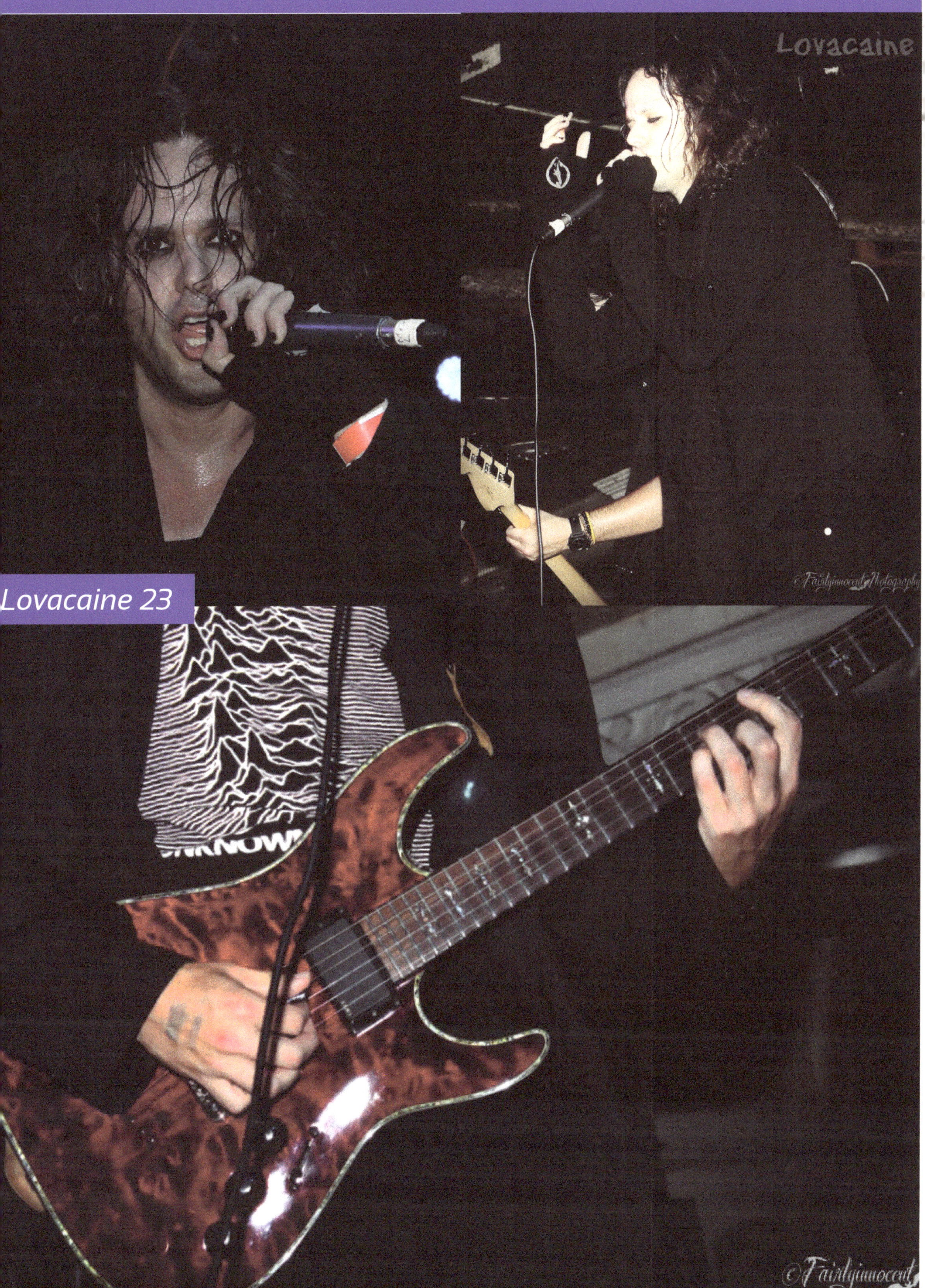
Lovacaine
Lovacaine 23
©Fairlyinnocent Photography
©Fairlyinnocent

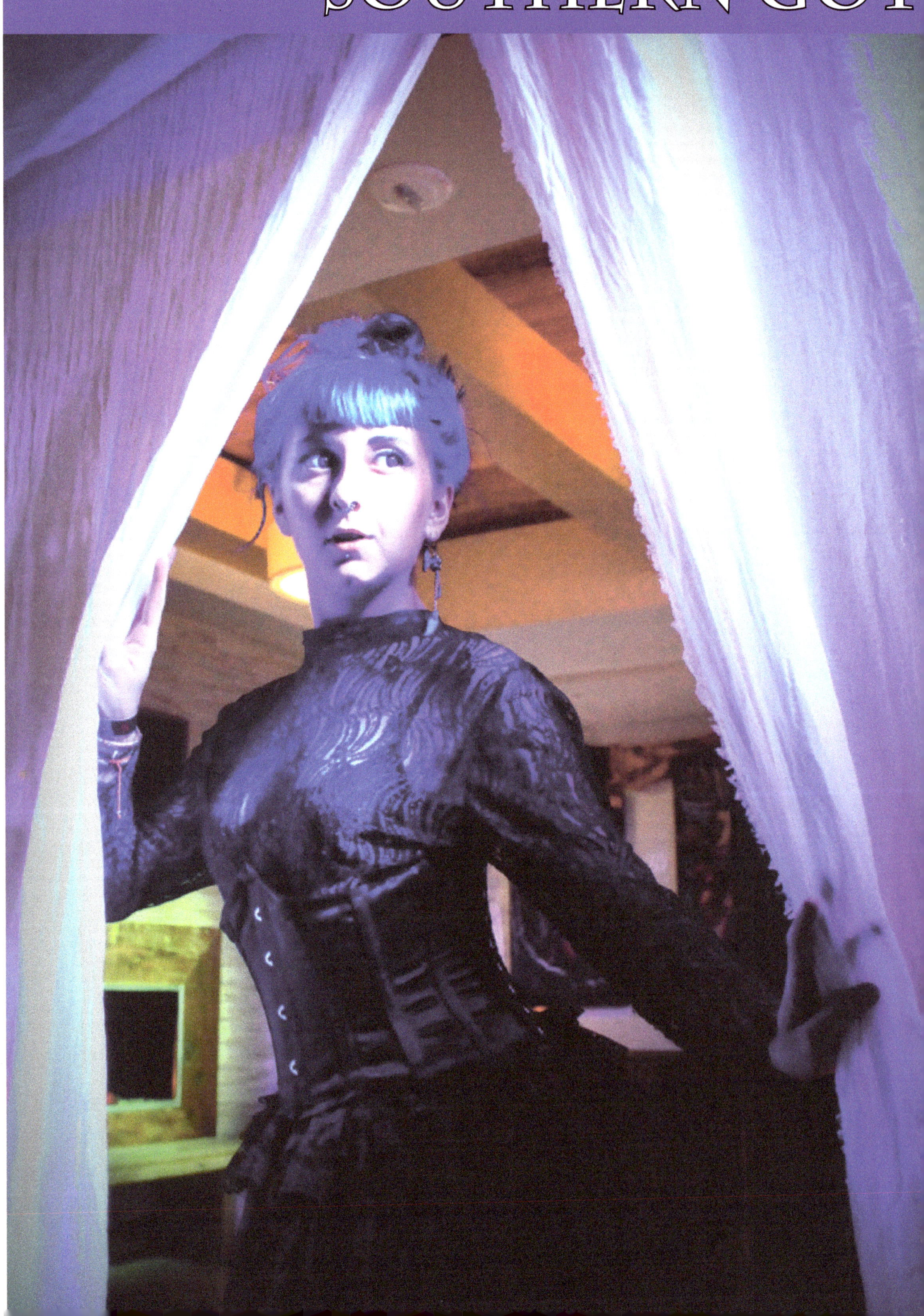

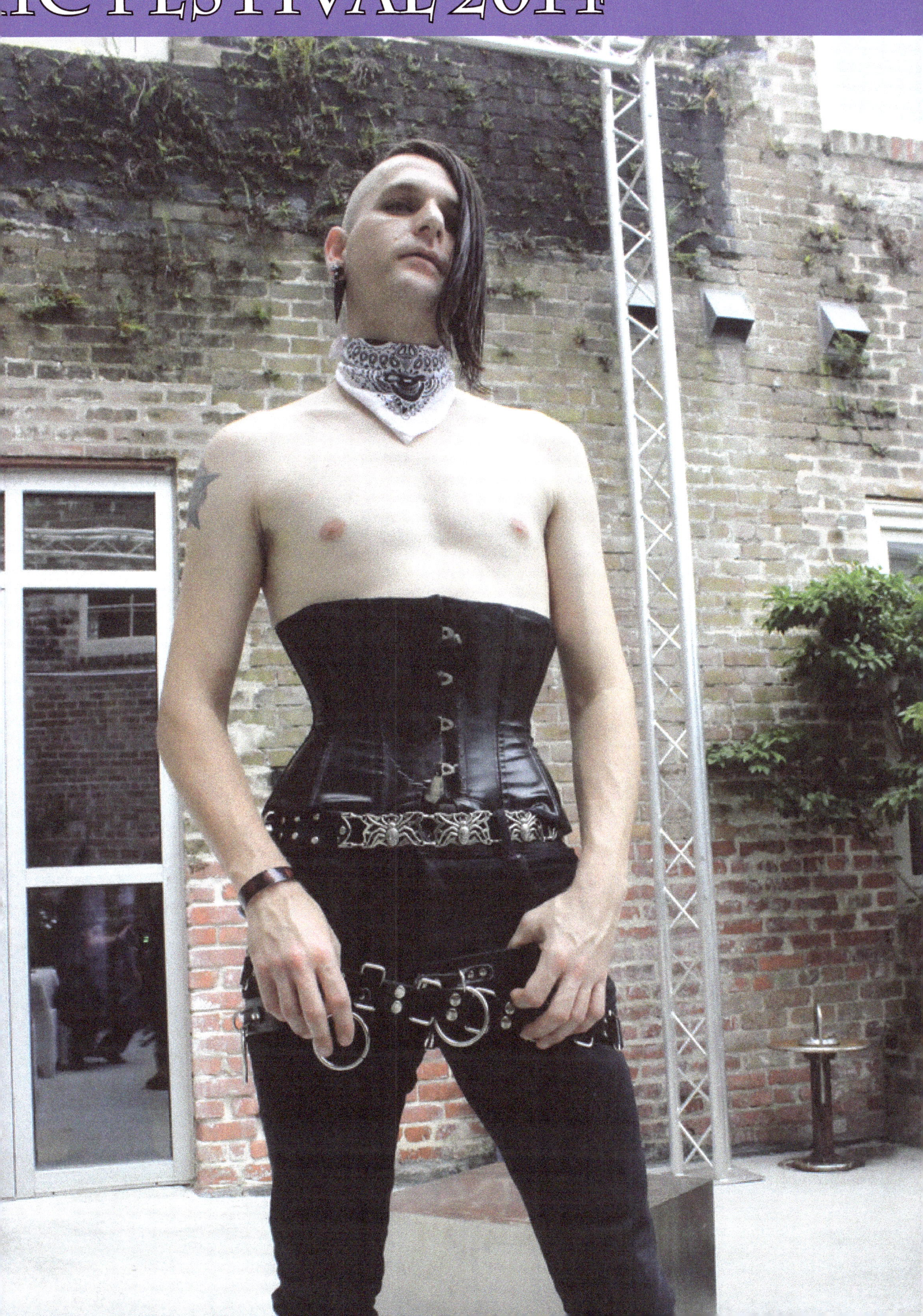

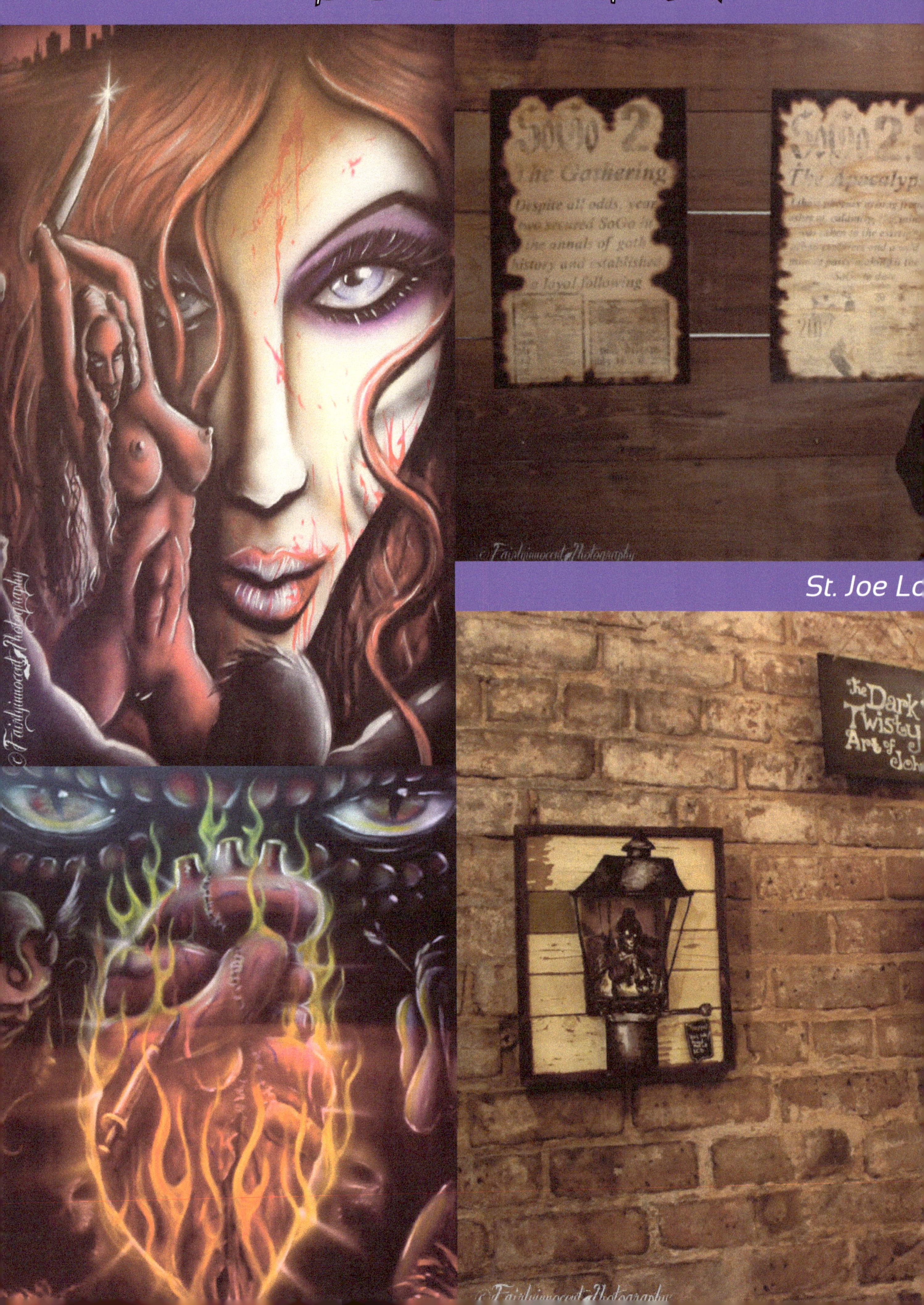
St. Joe Lo

IC FESTIVAL 2014

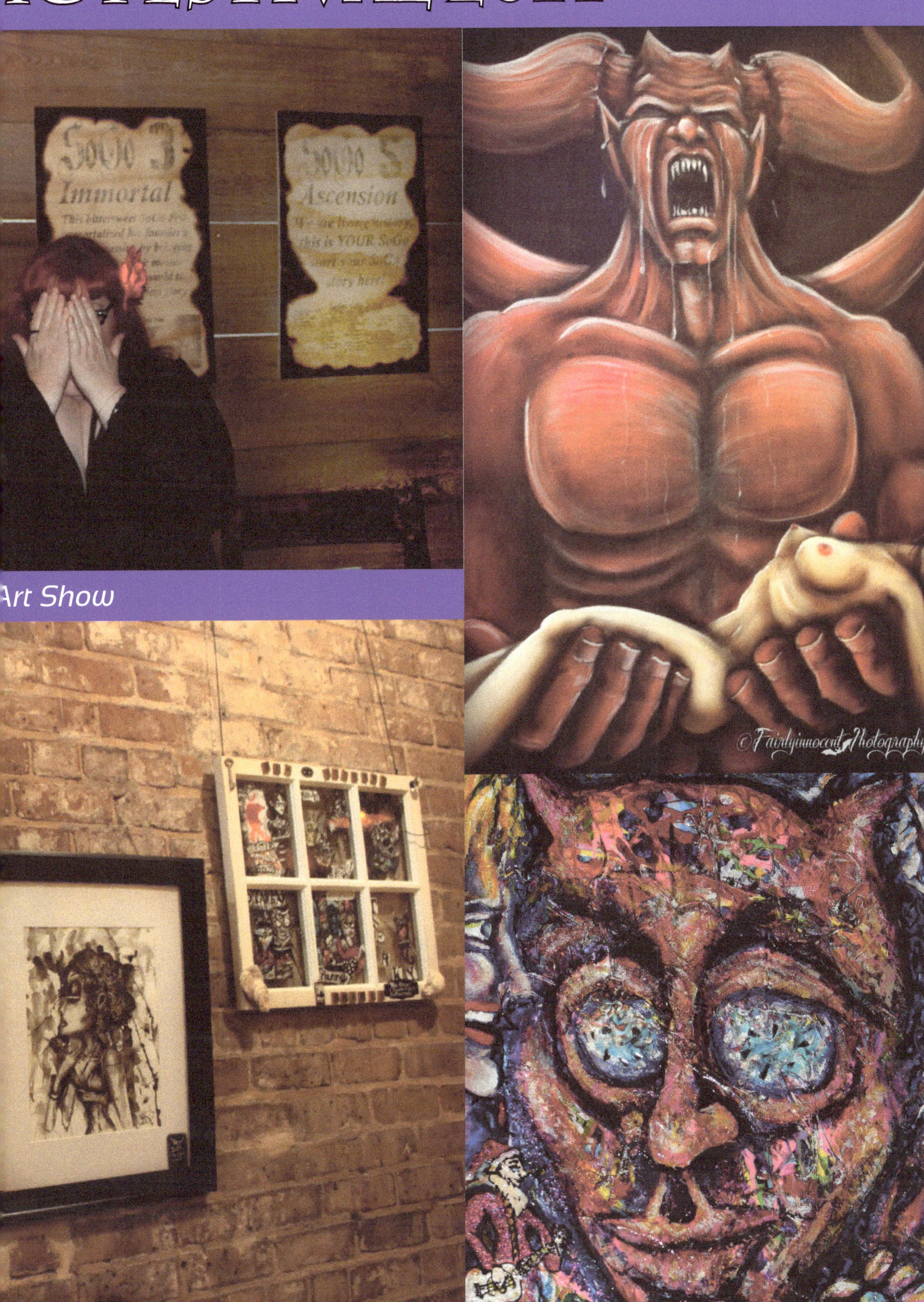

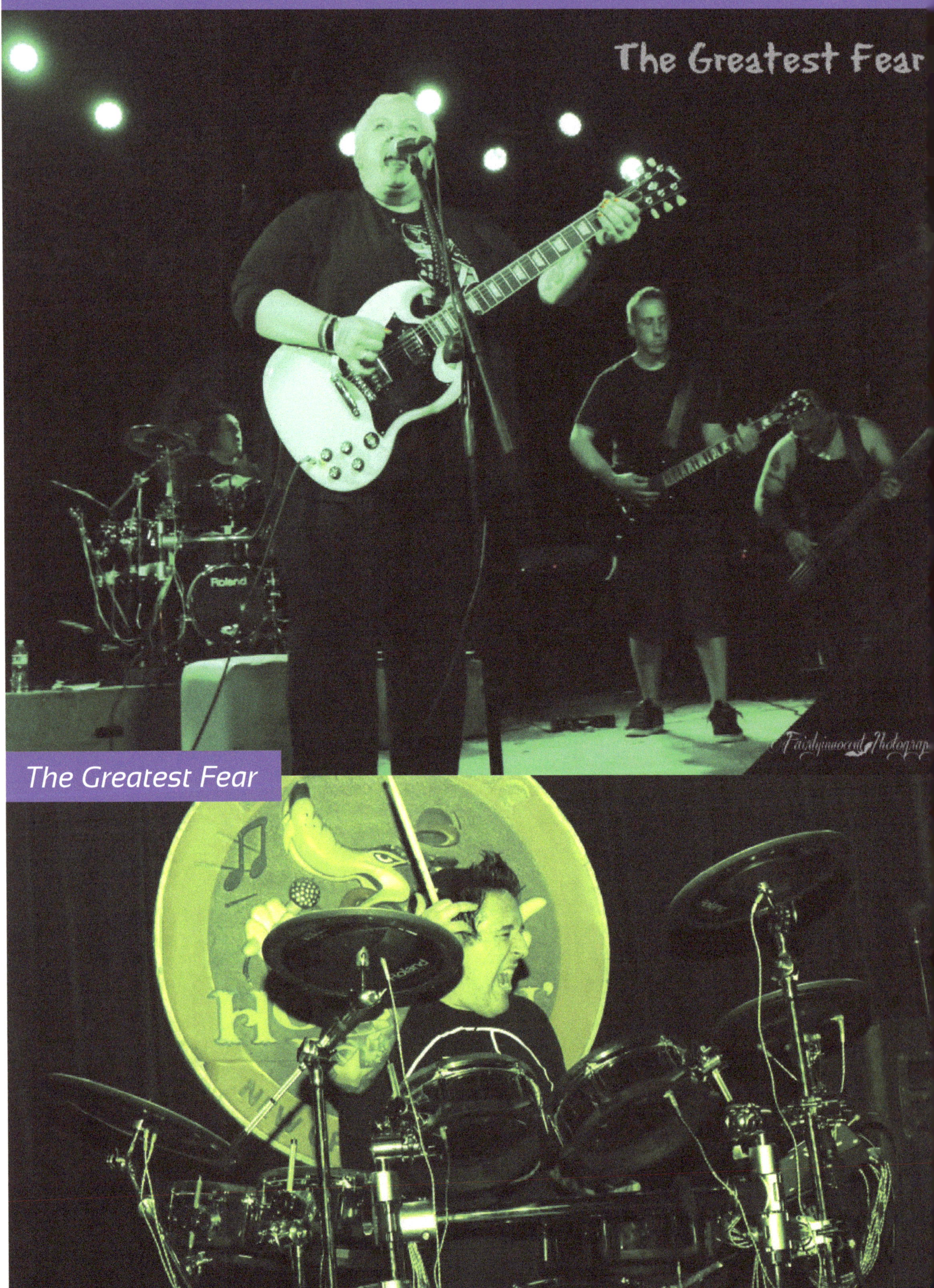
The Greatest Fear
The Greatest Fear

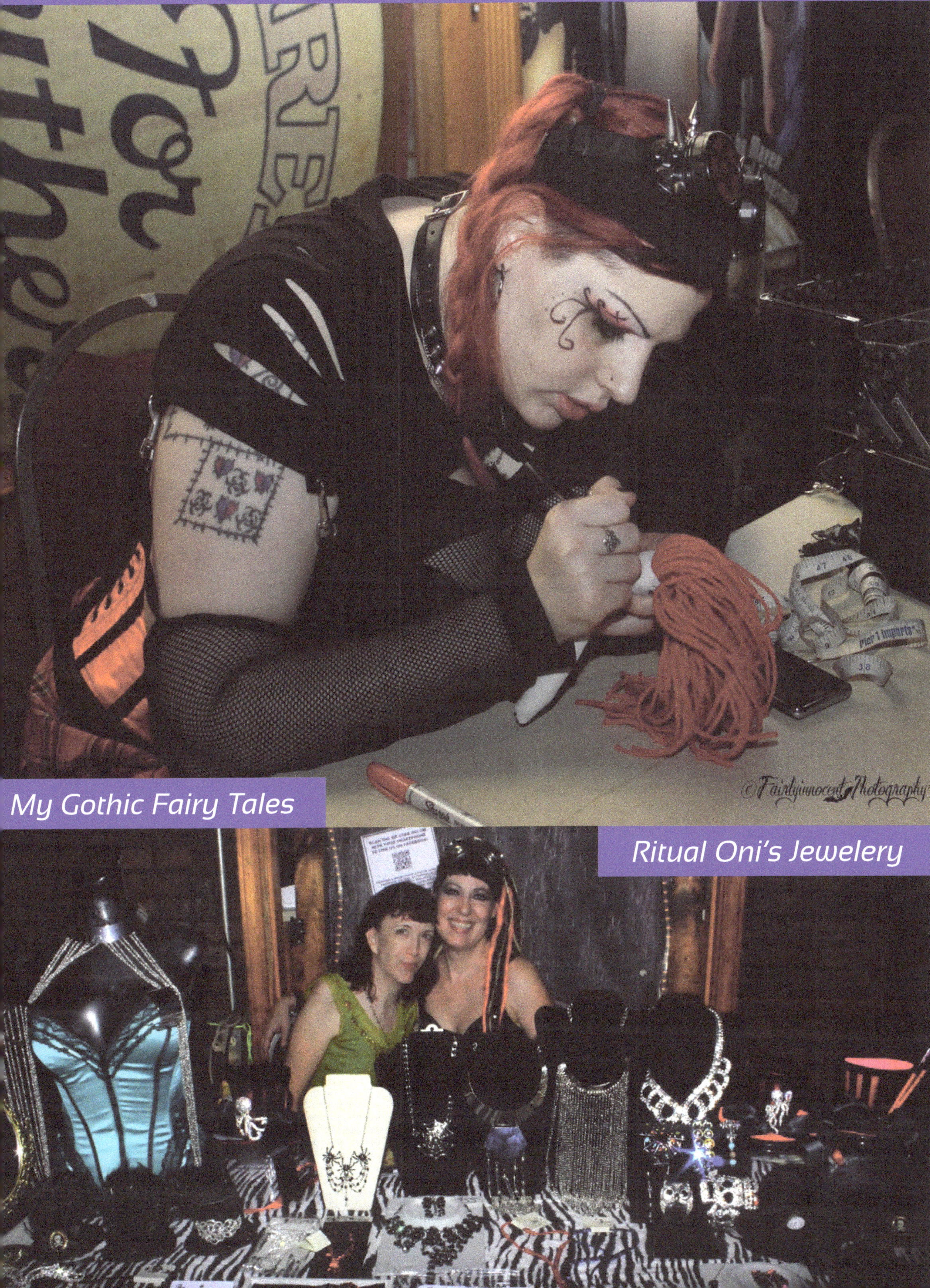

My Gothic Fairy Tales

Ritual Oni's Jewelery

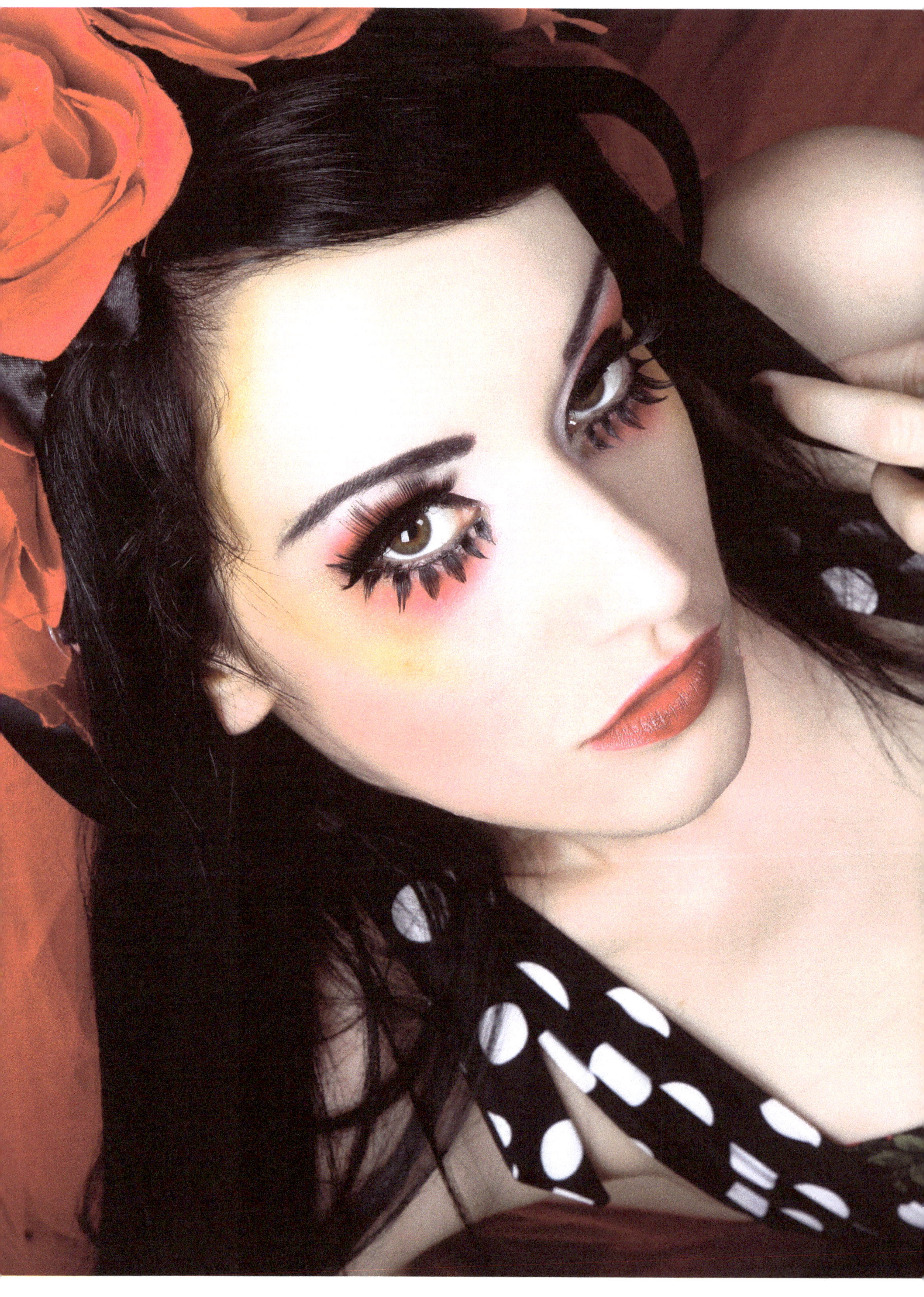

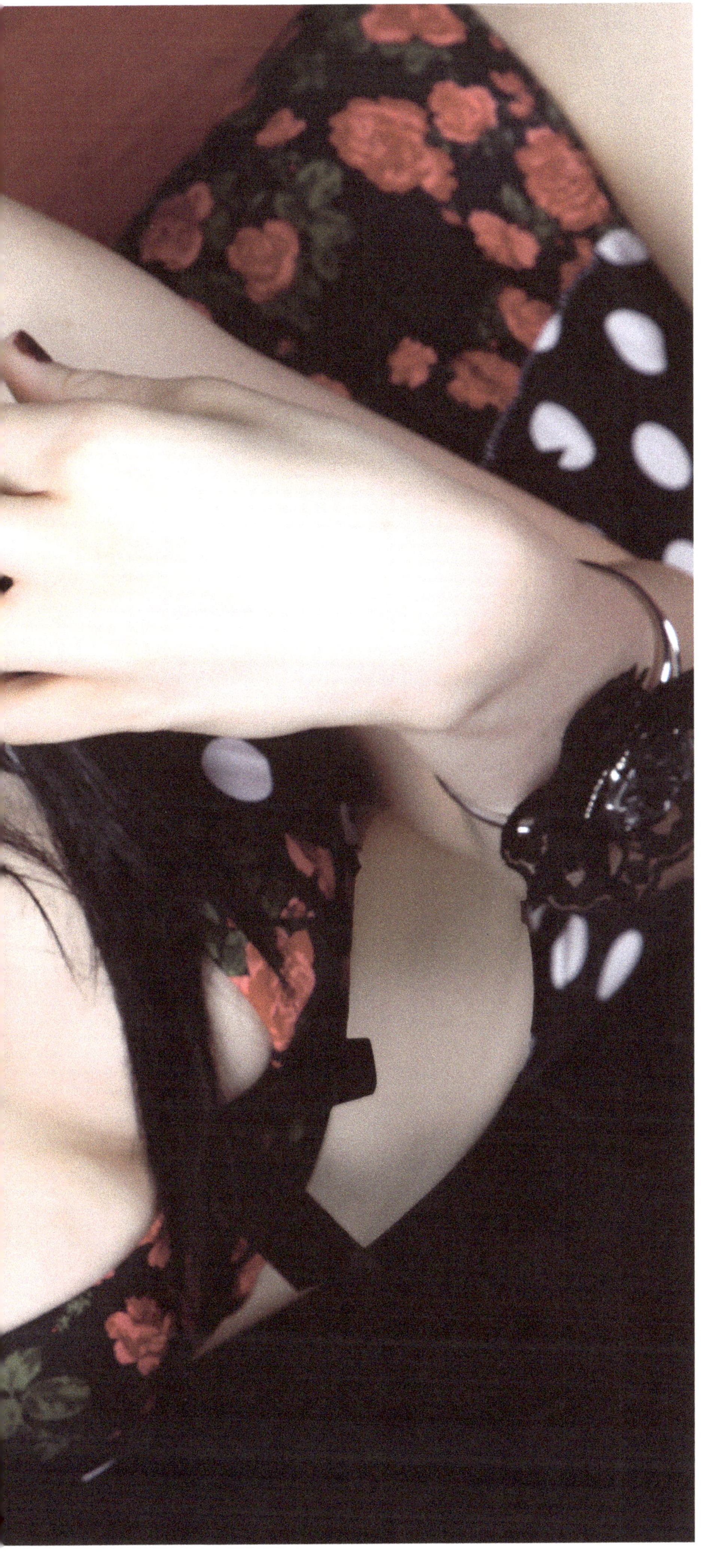

VALERIE GENTILE

Carpe Nocturne's interview.

By XXX ZOMBIEBOY XXX

XXX ZOMBIEBOY XXX: Hey Val thank you for taking the time to talk with us!

Valerie Gentile: Why thank you for having me! It's a pleasure and an honor.

ZB: Between music and modeling you are being quite prolific! What projects are you currently involved in?

VG: Right now I'm primarily focusing on my solo project. I'm an on call guitar player for Natalia Kills. I recorded guitar & sang on the track Serpent Crown by Everything Goes Cold off their new album Black Out the Sun, just released July 7th, 2014. I'm always opened for new projects however it's just been me and my music as of late.

ZB: Could you give us a little musical history perhaps? How you first got into guitar playing and singing?

VG: Well I always loved to sing. My mom would always have a top 40 radio station on every day while she were cleaning and making dinner. It made her really happy. She was always dancing around and singing along. So it ended up making me happy to hear the radio and dance around. From there on I just was inspired by what music can do and always wanted to pursue it.

ZB: Whom were your biggest influences?

VG: My mom, George Harrison, Wes Borland, Jem and the Holograms & Abbey Nex.

ZB: Could you tell us about Industrial Girl Bike Gang and how it came to be?

VG: An Angelspit tour got canceled in the spring of 2012 so Amelia and I set out to do our own thing. Which was partying and DJing. Possibly the most exciting thing I've ever done and got paid to do.

ZB: And Black Tape For A Blue Girl?

VG: I knew Athan Maroulis, singer of Black Tape for a Blue Girl, from when I was in The Cruxshadows. When I moved back to New York City he asked me to audition. Their current female singer and guitarist Nicki Jane was leaving the band and they were looking for a replacement for her. I was lucky enough to get the gig.

ZB: Can you tell us a little about what other bands you have either been in or collaborated with?

VG: Well I was in the Cruxshadows for about a year. That's where I caught my first big break into the Goth scene and touring. It was a lot of fun and I'm really grateful for the experience. They were my favorite band when I was in college. It's neat to be in your favorite band. I also played with Everything Goes Cold in their Fall 2012 tour. Which was my favorite band I've ever toured with. Good songs with great musicians with great attitudes.

ZB: Give us a run down of your choice of weapons in recording and performance if you would?

VG: I LOVE working in Protools. It's a good sounding DAW with my favorite set of editing tools. I kinda write songs along the way of recording & to have a good set of editing capabilities is key for me. I want things done fast before I forget what it was I was suppose to be doing! I like Ableton for DJing. I can't stand Logic. That program is not for me, even though I end up using it once a year for something that pops up. I just can't stand it. I get bummed out when I have to use it. It's great if you're a composer but that's not me. I've been into Dean Guitars lately. They seem louder to me then Gibsons and can take more of a beating. I really like Maschine by Native Instruments. For live, I like performing with a good ol' fashion Shure SM 58. Why? Because every other mic I tried out I have to hold too close to my lips for comfort to get the sound I want. I was very surprised. I like the Sennheiser 935's sound better but again I hate holding a mic super close to my face. My front teeth have enough chips in them from singing

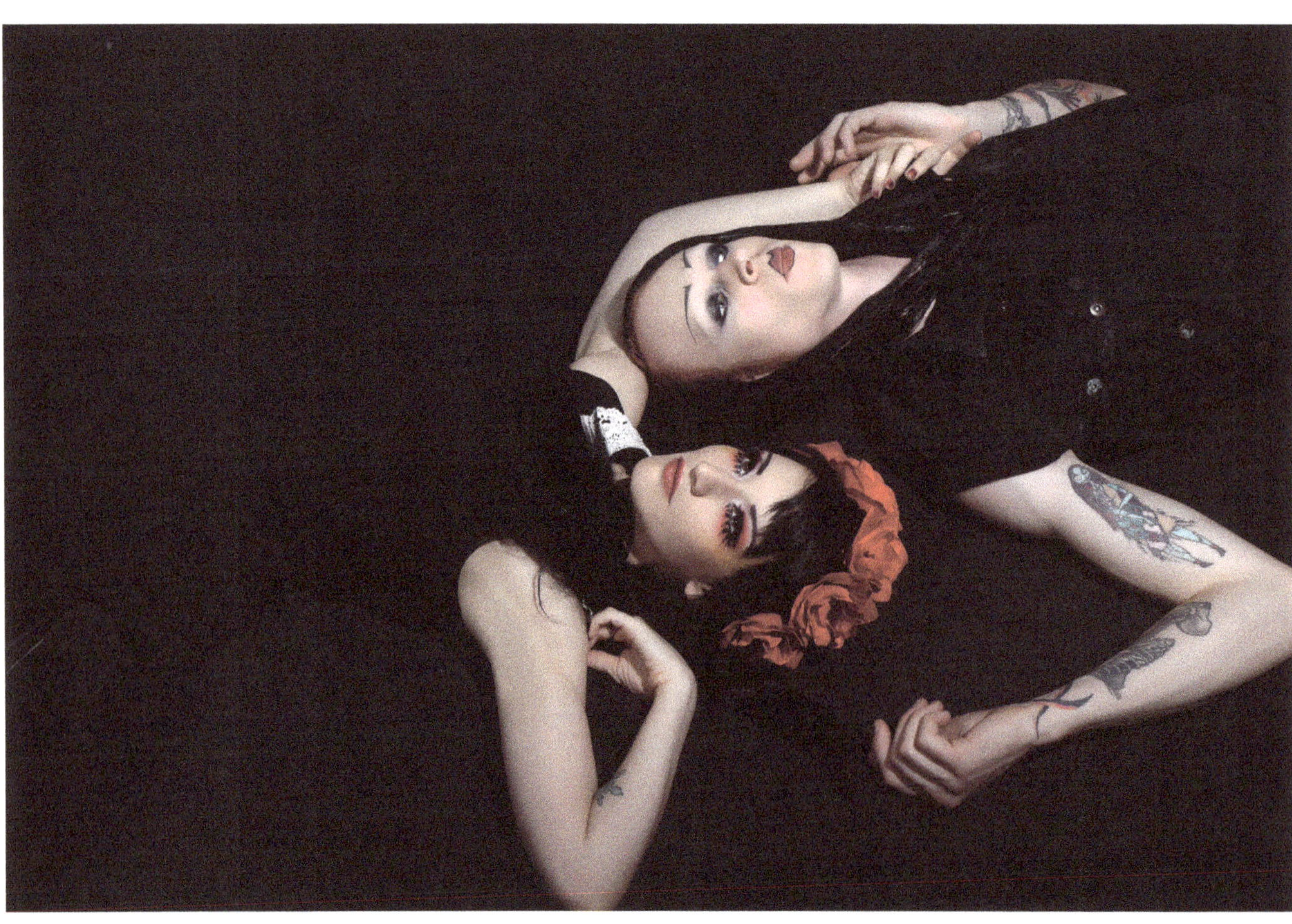

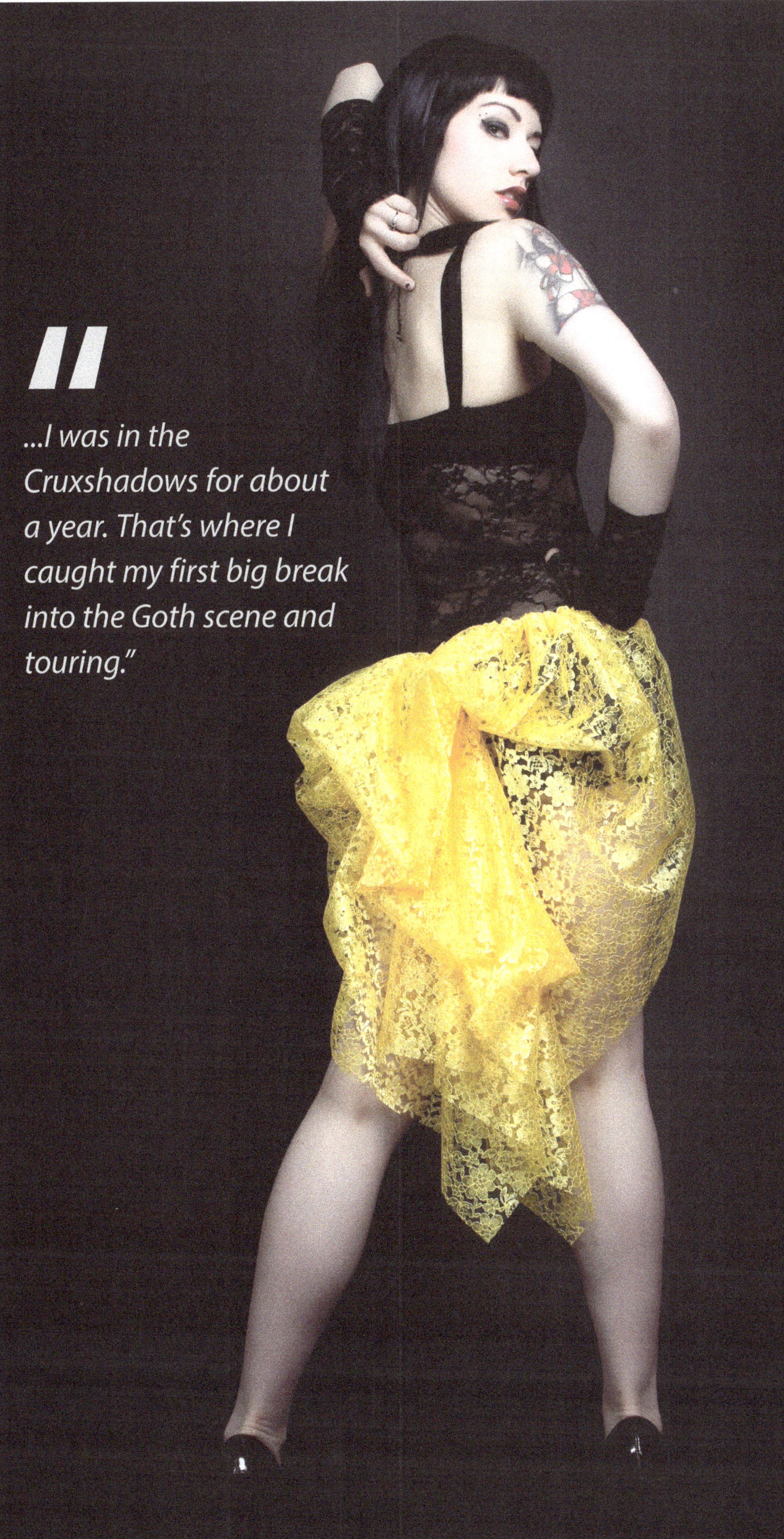

"

...I was in the
Cruxshadows for about
a year. That's where I
caught my first big break
into the Goth scene and
touring."

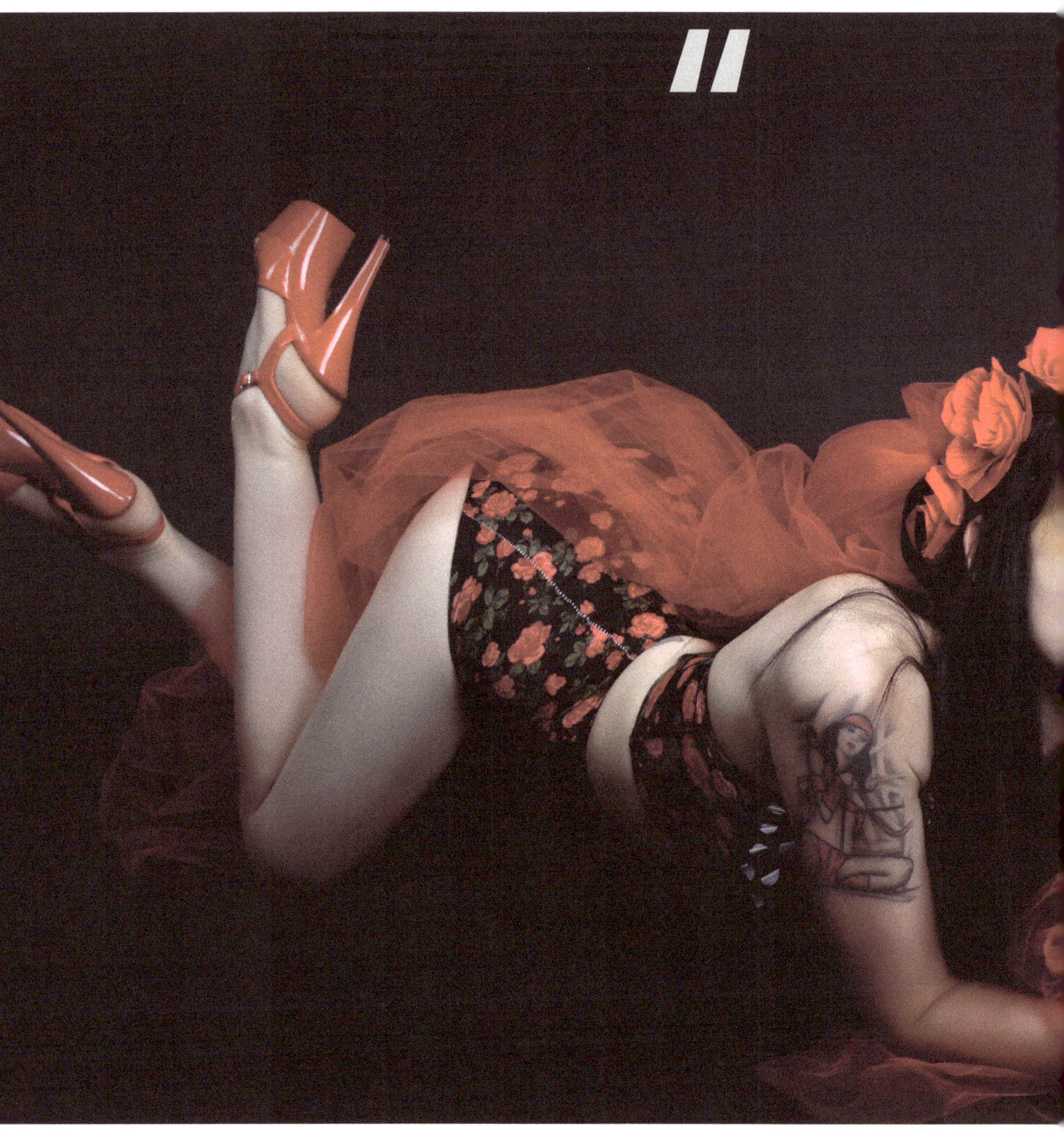

into mics like that.

ZB: What made you choose the guitar you are playing now?

VG: Right now I'm playing a Dean guitar. I have a love/hate relationship with it. Abbey Nex bought it for me the first Christmas we spent together. I'm lucky to have it. It sounds great and every time I plug it in I'm just impressed with what I hear. However, it so freaking heavy. After 20 minutes it wears me out, if I haven't played it in a while. It's the heaviest and most uncomfortable guitar I've ever played. However it is the best sounding by far & I like the way it looks on me.

ZB: What do you tend to do before a performance?

VG: I put 10 pounds of makeup on, stretch, ask my guitar to not break any strings, find stage towels, tape cables, pedal board, wireless transmitter & guitars picks in place and pray to the great George Harrison to make me awesome.

ZB: Are there any bands out there that you hope to either tour with or collaborate with in the future?

VG: Combichrist, Ayria and The Breakup

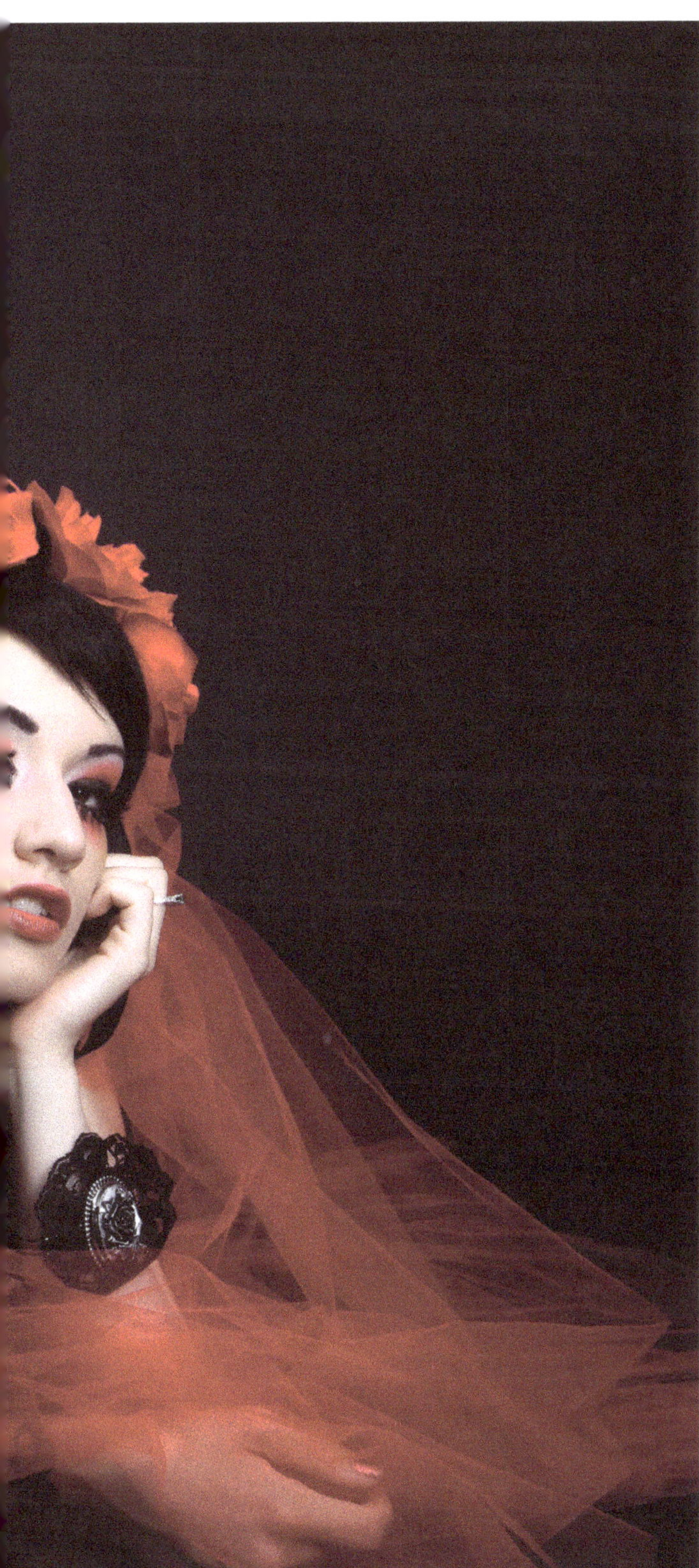

VG: I moved back to New York, after living in Hollywood for a year, and have a few close friends that happen to be photographers. Two of them being Candylust and d. yee. Both base out of Brooklyn and we live fairly close to each other.

ZB: Are there any photographers you particularly like working with or hope to?

VG: I would really like to work again with Jane Queen aka Dangerously Dolly & Michelle Star. Jane Queen shot the pictures I was in for the Angelspit album Hello My Name Is & The Industrial Girl Bike Gang promo pictures. Michelle Star shot pictures for an A is for Arsenic clothing line that Amelia Arsenic, Ashley from News Year Day and myself were a part of.

ZB: Aside from modeling and music do you have any other artistic endeavors?

VG: I like crocheting! I just started getting into that. I also would like to get into candle and soap making… when I have the time and a real stove.

ZB: Tell us if you would, a little about your EP album Love Is Luxury.

VG: It's a collection of 4 songs about the year I lived in heartbreak in the land of North Hollywood, California. Glad that's over. I feel like that era of my life is so over. I'm ready to write new music that reflects my life now!

ZB: You seem to have a thing for red?

VG: I wanted to be Sailor Mars when I grew up. Her favorite color is red. So it became mine! Heh heh. That and it looks pretty good on me, I think.

ZB: I would also like to take a moment to congratulate you on your upcoming marriage!

VG: Thank you! I'm looking forward to it & becoming Mrs. Nex!

ZB: Where did you meet Abbey Nex?

VG: When I was playing guitar for Angelspit we were supporting Combichrist for a couple of shows on their tour. The first show we played with them was in Baltimore, May of 2011. I met Abbey then. I remember wanting to talking to him and telling Amelia I thought he was cute but I never had the courage to talk to him. The summer of 2012 I was djing a show with Off With Her Head in Orange County, California and Abbey was playing that same show with the band The Witch Was Right. We finally started talking during the show rehearsal the night before, since we

ZB: Your video for Scarred just came out in June. Would you share with us a little about how it was created and what went into it?

VG: I wanted to do a video for Scarred since I released the Love is Luxury EP. My best friend from childhood, d. yee pretty much wrote the concept and shot it. I love working with her. She also did the So Far Away promo video and all the artwork for the Love is Luxury EP.

ZB: You've been doing a lot of modeling lately as well. What got you into doing that?

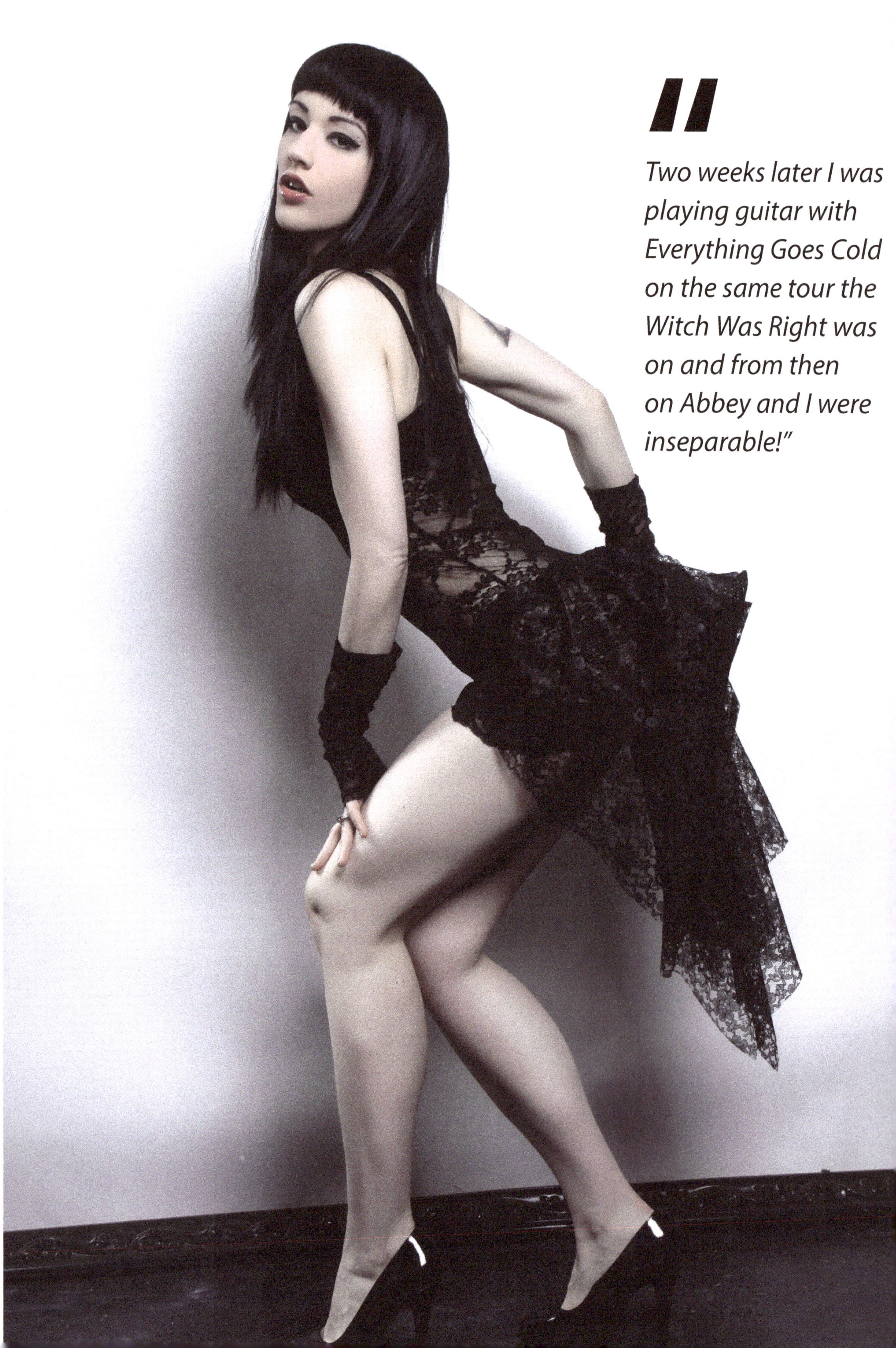

"

Two weeks later I was
playing guitar with
Everything Goes Cold
on the same tour the
Witch Was Right was
on and from then
on Abbey and I were
inseparable!"

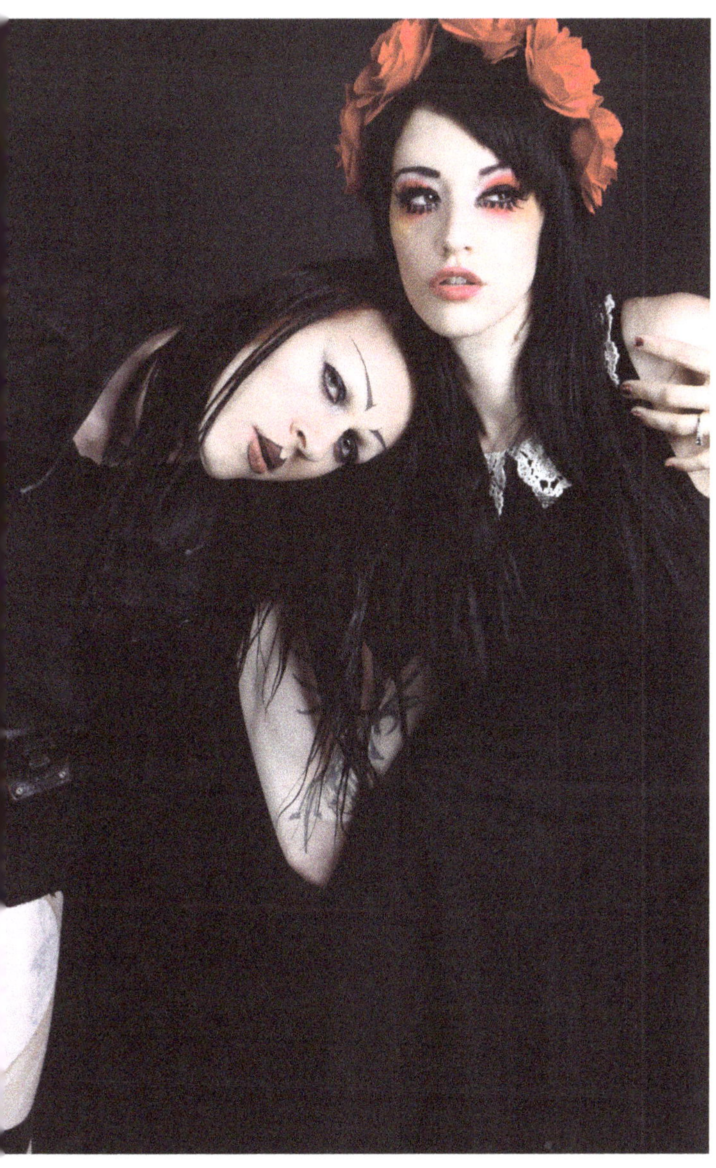

shared the same rehearsal spot. Two weeks later I was playing guitar with Everything Goes Cold on the same tour the Witch Was Right was on and from then on Abbey and I were inseparable!

ZB: Was collaboration immediate or did it evolve?

VG: It evolved once Ted Phelps of Imperative Reaction had us be bench buddies in the van for tour we were on. Thank you Ted!

ZB: Favorite zombie killing weapon and why? Go!

VG: Metal bat. Easy to take a zombie's head off with one. I could also swing it faster than I could reload a shotgun. However I wouldn't turn down a loaded shotgun or anything I could take a zombie's head off with.

ZB: I'm with you on the bat, though I prefer wood even though it is not as strong. Just something about the feel of a Louisville Slugger! I see your current occupation as Duke of New York "A Number One"! You can call me Snake. Carpenter fan?

VG: I get that a lot. People think I'm dead.

ZB: What other artists, musicians and filmmakers do you draw influence from or just enjoy?

VG: James Rolfe aka the Angry Video Game Nerd is probably the biggest inspiration in my life.

ZB: I met that man outside of the Ghostbusters headquarters in New York once while he was filming! Super nice guy and he interviewed me and my friends!

VG: He is a true example of doing what you love and never giving up. I wish up an eternity of success & happiness.

ZB: And modeling inspirations?

VG: PINTEREST!

ZB: And you seem a bit of a gamer as well?

VG: Yes! I love most fighting & adventure games. Favorite games of all time: Chrono Trigger, The Street Fighter Games, Fire Ensemble (gamecube and wii versions only), The Hitman games, Soul Calibur series and the Zelda games. I think the newest game I like is Bayonetta.

ZB: Tell us what's next for Valerie Gentile other than raising an army dead ravens out of a pit in the desert to lead them to total world domination?

VG: I should really finish writing an album so I can go on tour to take over the world... but if not the world then just peoples MP3 players.

FIN

(Photo credits: Candylust Photography)

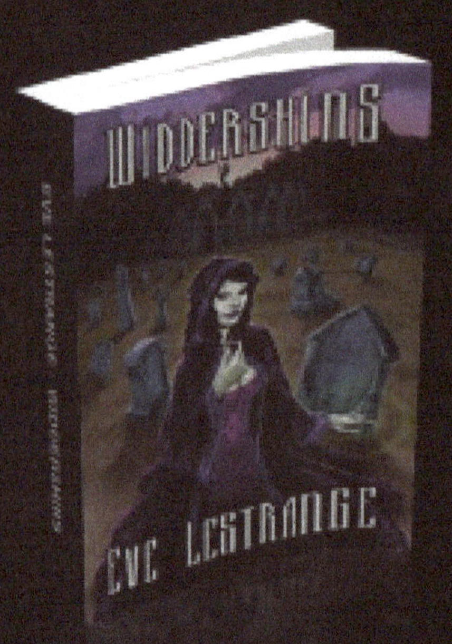

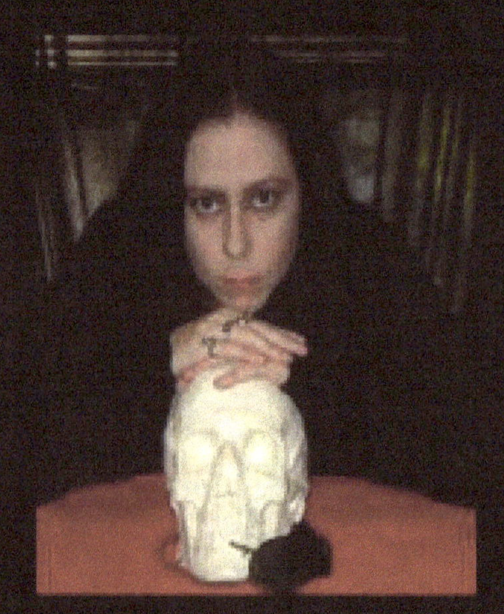

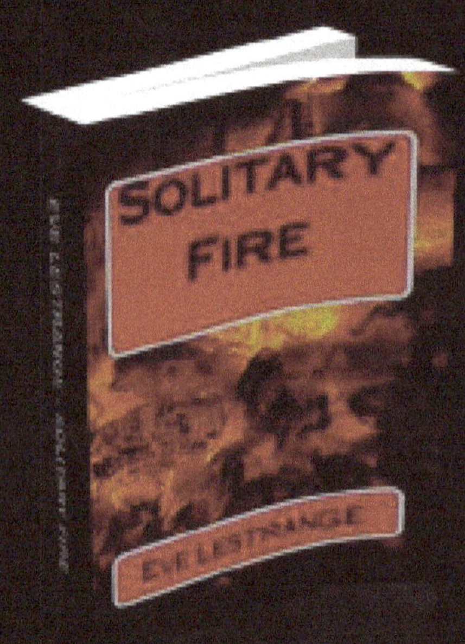

GOTHIC HORROR IS BACK ... WITH A VENGEANCE!

DELVE INTO THE PROVOCATIVE WORLD OF BLACK MAGIC AND THE OCCULT WITH THESE SPELL-BINDING NOVELS FROM AUTHOR, EVE LESTRANGE. FOLLOW 18TH CENTURY SORCERESS, CHRISTINA LAFAGE DOWN THE LEFT-HANDED PATH AND BEYOND AS SHE SELLS HER SOUL FOR THE FIERCE POWER OF THE BLACK ARTS. ENTER CHRISTINA'S WORLD AND JOIN HER ADVENTURES IN SPELL CASTING AND DARK DEEDS.

WIDDERSHINS INTRODUCES A STRONG FEMALE CHARACTER INTO THE HORROR GENRE–CHRISTINA LAFAGE, AN EIGHTEENTH CENTURY FRENCH GIRL WHO SELLS HER SOUL FOR THE FIERCE POWER OF THE BLACK ARTS. CHRISTINA'S WORLD IS FILLED WITH SPELL CASTING, BLACK MAGIC, DISTANT LANDS AND INTENSE POWER. THE STORY UNFOLDS WITH CHRISTINA'S INTRODUCTION INTO THE BLACK ARTS BY A MYSTERIOUS BENEFACTOR THAT SHE MEETS IN A WOODED GROVE. THIS BENEFACTOR, MADAME DUCHAMP, TAKES CHRISTINA UNDER HER WING AND TEACHES HER TO USE THE POWERS OF THE OCCULT AND BEND THE LAWS OF NATURE TO HER WILL AS THEY PROVIDE SPELLS AND SERVICES FOR THE WEALTHY ARISTOCRATS OF PARIS. AT FIRST SHE STRUGGLES WITH HER NEWLY ACQUIRED POWER AND WITH HER OWN FEELINGS OF DOUBT AND APPREHENSION UNTIL A GRAVE SITUATION FORCES HER TO CONQUER FEAR AND DOUBT. CHRISTINA'S POWER CONTINUES TO GROW AND EXPLODES INTO AN ELECTRIFYING SERIES OF EVENTS THAT LEAD HER TO EGYPT WHERE HER POWER IS PUT TO THE ULTIMATE TEST.

SOLITARY FIRE CONTINUES TO FOLLOW CHRISTINA LAFAGE ALONG THE LEFT HANDED PATH TO VIENNA WHERE WEALTHY NOBLEMAN, PAUL MRZAK PROMISES HER AND MADAME DUCHAMP UNIMAGINABLE RICHES AND A STRING OF AFFLUENT CLIENTS AT HIS CASTLE IN HUNGARY. PAUL'S CASTLE OFFERS MUCH INTRIGUE AND DECEPTION THAT FEEDS CHRISTINA'S OWN SUSPICIONS ABOUT PAUL'S TRUE MOTIVE BEHIND HIS GENEROUS INVITATION. CHRISTINA'S POWER CONTINUES TO BLOSSOM AND FASCINATE THE NOBLES OF PAUL'S COURT, WHO FLOCK TO HER FOR ALL MANNERS OF OCCULT SERVICES. BUT IT IS PAUL'S OWN REQUEST AND THE PROMISE OF A SUBSTANTIAL FORTUNE THAT LEAD CHRISTINA DEEPER INTO THE BLACK ARTS WHERE STRANGE VISIONS AND FEELINGS OF DESTINY HAUNT HER DREAMS. MEANWHILE PAUL'S PLAN BEGINS TO UNRAVEL, BRINGING SINISTER SECRETS TO LIGHT. HOWEVER IT IS NOT ONLY PAUL HARBORING SECRETS AS CHRISTINA CONFRONTS HER MASTER, LUCIEN, ABOUT HER INTENSIFYING VISIONS. CAN THE INTIMACY THAT SHE AND LUCIEN HAVE COME TO SHARE PREPARE CHRISTINA FOR THE WHOLE SHOCKING TRUTH?

BOTH BOOKS AVAILABLE NOW AT WWW.AMAZON.COM.
FOLLOW EVE ON FACEBOOK: WWW.FACEBOOK.COM/EVE.LESTRANGE
& SCRIBD: WWW.SCRIBD.COM/EVELESTRANGE6632
& WWW.EVELESTRANGE.COM

Parisian Gothic Death Rock from The Cemetary Girlz!

By LinnieSarah (@linnieloowho)

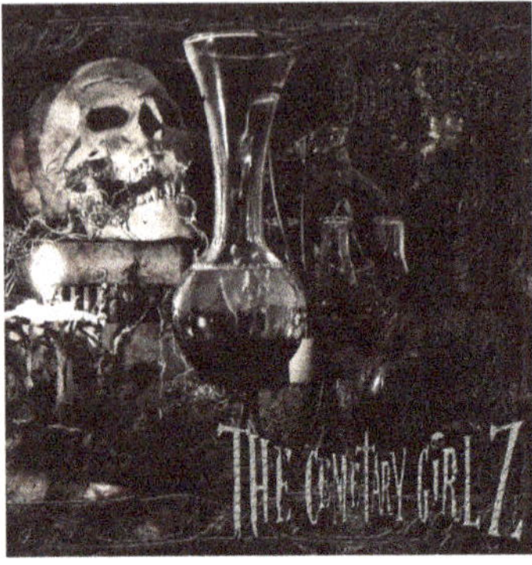

Parisian Gothic Death Rock: it's not a common genre by any means, but that's what makes it so intriguing! Based out of Paris (obviously), The Cemetary Girlz are a four-piece gothic rock band with a list of influences a mile long. But if you love classic horror, Gothic literature, giallos, B-movies, and Tim Burton, then you will love the music of The Cemetary Girlz.

Released in June of 2013, The Cemetary Girlz's album, Opus Vitae, is a 14-track journey into the macabre. Many of the songs give the feeling of wandering in a haze through the catacombs of Paris, which is appropriate given, that's the location the band claims as their hometown. You can absolutely see these songs soundtracking a supernatural heavy metal horror movie... A good heavy metal horror though: not the painfully self-aware, "trying too hard" kind.

I love the international flair to the tracks on Opus Vitae. It's not just that the lyrics are in French; it's that they actually have the feel of a classic foreign horror film like Nosferatu.

Something dark and dangerous but beautiful and classic. The song "Dracula is Cannibal" is actually reminiscent of something you'd hear on a midnight monster show hosted by Vampyra. It's fun and silly but still creepy and sure to satisfy any horror lover.

If you're interested in the dark gothic vibes of The Cemetary Girlz, you can find their album (along with previews of all the songs) at http://thecemetarygirlz.bandcamp.com/. Don't miss out on your chance to discover this fascinating band before everyone else does!

VRIL
VIOLET CARSON

Label: Dunkelheit
2008
Electro-dark, synth-pop

by Sergio Manghina

I didn't know anything about this band, but they were a trio from Santa Cruz de Tenerife, Spain. Anyway, their name comes from an esoteric book written in 1870 by Edward Bulwer-Lytton and titled Vril: The Power of the Coming Race, where Vril is a mysterious energetic substance able to give psychic powers.
On this debut album , Alaya, Varick and Midian work with an elastic definition of electro-goth influenced by the whole '80s synth-pop tradition.

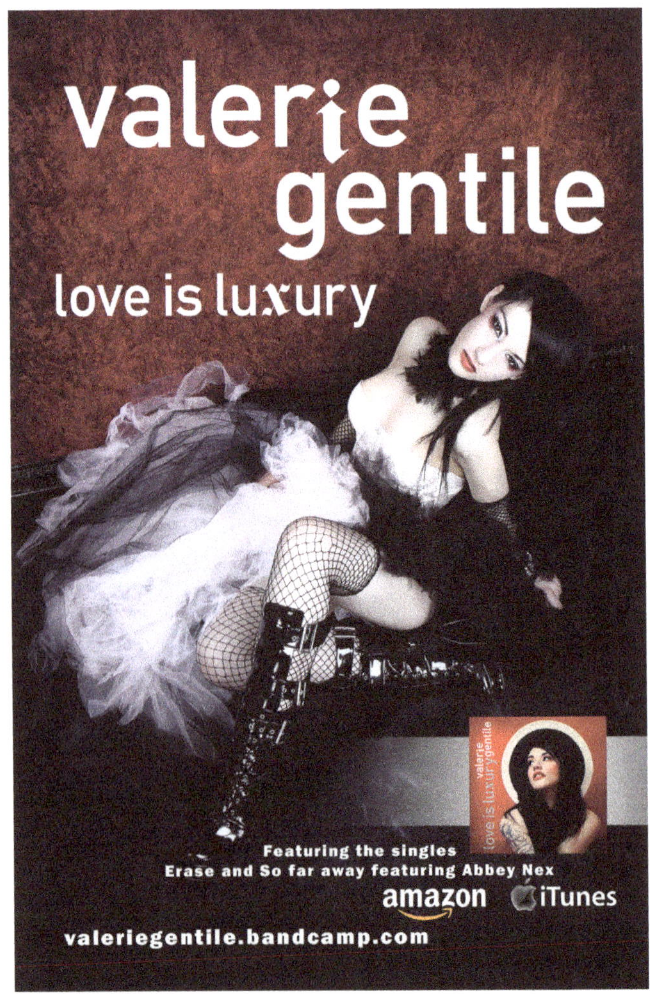

"Angels Also Can Kiss" is a phantasmagoric magic-box unpacked by two beautiful female voices, crossing each other's path, while the ethereal "Behind The Mask" flows among an amniotic synth fluid. This song, as well as other pieces on the disc ("Dear World" and "Dark Forest") reminds me of some Italian electro-dance experiences like Planet Funk, and part of the collection, sounds slightly influenced by various artists based in Italy, more than whatever British or German pattern of reference. Therefore, I suppose that this can happen only deep down inside on a subconscious level. This impression is due to the peculiar mediterranean flavour that pervades the electro-dance heart of these tracks, displaying an extensive knowledge of various aspects of Italian music, integrated with another kind of subliminal input (Evanescence). This is still more evident in tracks like "Aabye", a neo classical piece sung in fluent Italian and inspired - in some way- by Italo-prog, or in the dramatic "Laboratorio estrano".

Catchy and captivating, Vril combines a good fusion of many different stimuli avoiding trivial slips and maintaining a constant route.

ACRETONGUE
"Strange Cargo"
Label: Metropolis Records
Release Date: November 15th, 2011
Rating: 5 stars

By Anthony McCracken

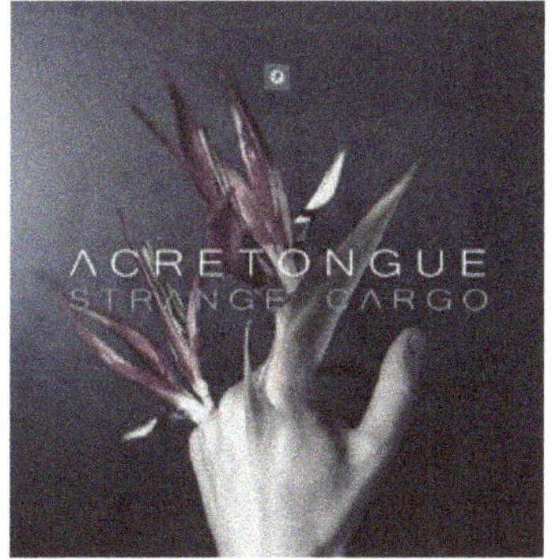

For Christmas last year I was given some of the best headphones I've ever come across. Knowing what these headphones were capable of, I couldn't wait to hear all of my music collection with them. But the first album I chose to experience in this fashion was "Strange Cargo" by Acretongue. Not because they come early in the alphabet on my iTunes, but because it's one of the most sonically gorgeous albums I've heard.

Acretongue layers a lot of beautiful sounds over each other in gradual build-ups that create a whole other world. A lot of bands seem to come up with a really good beat and great EBM and insert vocals into it but Acretongue's songs feel equally built around vocals and lyrics as they do the music. If you're a fan of Haujobb or De/Vision, or if you haven't gotten into the more atmospheric sides of electronic music, be sure to check out "Strange Cargo."

"Unspoken" is probably the best place to start, where the song takes its time a little more and you can hear the variety of sounds in a more individualized setting before they combine. "Origin" is little more fast-paced with a brooding drone carrying the lighter and ominous sounds. The album's title track is one that hides a creeping sense of unease in the combination of small sounds that feed off each other to drive home the tone that was building all along: that there's something inside of you watching and waiting. Lyrics and sound rarely marry in such perfect focus as they do here. Acretongue provides the lyrics on their website, and after listening to the album a number of times before reading them it can give the experience a chilling new dimension.

MENTAL DISCIPLINE
"Butterfly EP"
Label: SkyQode
Release Date: March 20th,
2014
Rating: 4 stars

By Anthony McCracken

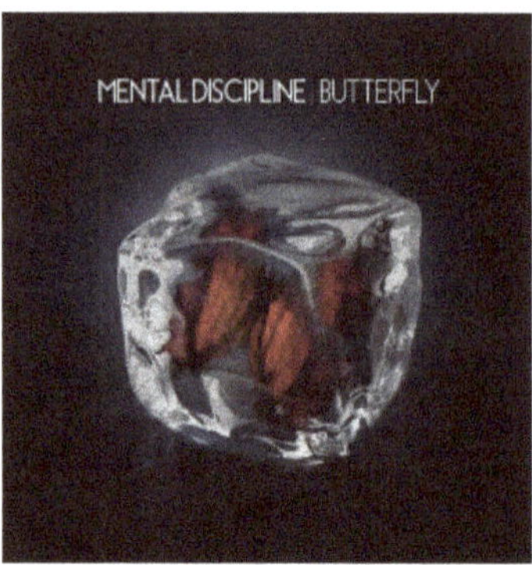

PREVERSE
"Obstacles"
Label: NYX Records
Release Date: April 25th,
2014
Rating: 5 stars

By Anthony McCracken

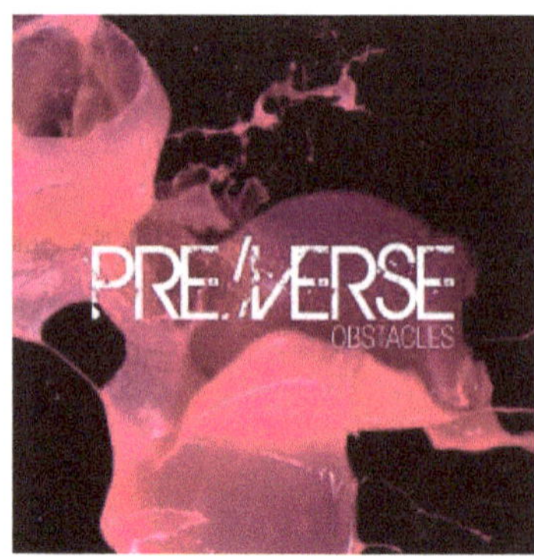

Russian Futurepop artist Mental Discipline has finally given a taste of their upcoming follow-up to their 2012 debut full-length "Constellation." "Butterfly" keeps a fast and catchy pace from start to finish in the fashion of some of Neuroticfish's best. Since "Constellation" featured the vocals of so many other musicians, it's nice that "Butterfly" is done without a guest vocalist. The production is incredible polished as one comes to expect with Mental Discipline and it only serve to raise anticipation for the album it will come from.

Next up is "Precious Paradise" remixed by Mind.In.A.Box and it's got to be one of the coolest songs released this year. The vocals are vocoder processed and the track certainly builds after the piano-driven intro. Stefan Poiss of Mind.In.A.Box contributes amazing vocals to give a real treat for fans of his projects. Then comes "Give Me a Memory" featuring vocals by Tess. This song is really just a redo of "God & Devil" with her vocals over it instead of Cold In May's. I love the original so much, this version is good but it doesn't come close to the other (which had been a standout to me).

Unity One remixed "Butterfly" and it rivals the original. They added a bit more depth to it and brought the emotion more, it's a stunning remix that does the song justice while adding a new dimension. The EP ends with "Until the End" (exclusive to this release) and it's a beautiful, slower song that reminds me of Seabound and finishes it nicely. It's the perfect EP to hold fans over until the bigger, full-length set to come out before the end of 2014.

"Obstacles" is the debut album from the German five-piece that combines synth-pop and EBM with a more rock feel to the structures of their songs. They've managed to combine guitars with electronic music in a much more seamless style than most. The album manages to be quite dark and brooding while keeping an energetic pace and even some frequent pop moments.

Some of the standout tracks are their darker ones like the opener "No Faith in My God" where the song builds from small eerie sounds to a booming chorus that makes losing faith sound like something to dance to. "My Shadow Has a Gun" reminds me of Unheilig or Rammstein with their verses but keep their own style with their melodic and open chorus. Preverse's use of guitars and live drums along with synths and fairly versatile vocals are all put to a variety of uses with each song and it's what makes the album so repeatable. Where they get dark and gloomy, they show their energy. When they lean more towards rock, they don't stick firmly to rock and bring in unexpected sounds.

"Trace of Water" starts out sounding like the band Dismantled but brings in Preverse's rock-sounding chorus among the EBM feel of the whole song giving something very melodic. "Truth Hurts" sounds like a perfect performance song for the band where everyone kicks into high gear from constant and quick synths to pounding drums and guitars that pack more power than most electronic bands show. Then we get "Rubbertears" that would be welcome to most Skinny Puppy fans in the vocal production and interesting lyrics that give some of the best verses on the album. "Bringing Me Home" feels like their take on a "Black Celebration"-era Depeche Mode style. With such a strong variety, this album has something for any mood which is no easy feat for a debut.

RUINED CONFLICT
"Revolutionary Mayhem"
Label: Ruined Conflict
Release Date: June 27th, 2014
Rating: 4 stars

By Anthony McCracken

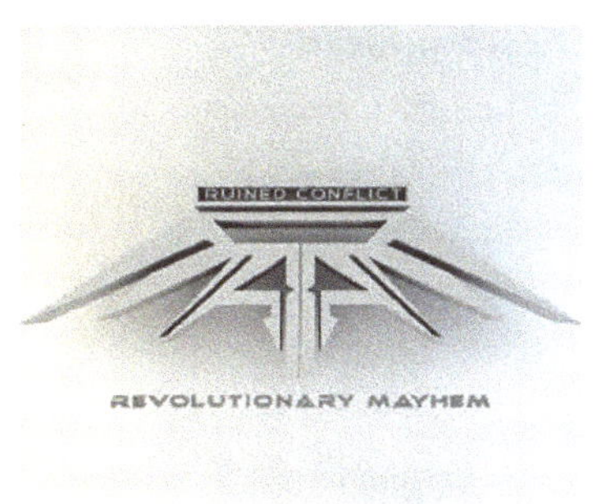

SLAVE REPUBLIC
"Quest For Love"
Label: Accession Records
Release Date: February 15th, 2013
Rating: 5 stars

By Anthony McCracken

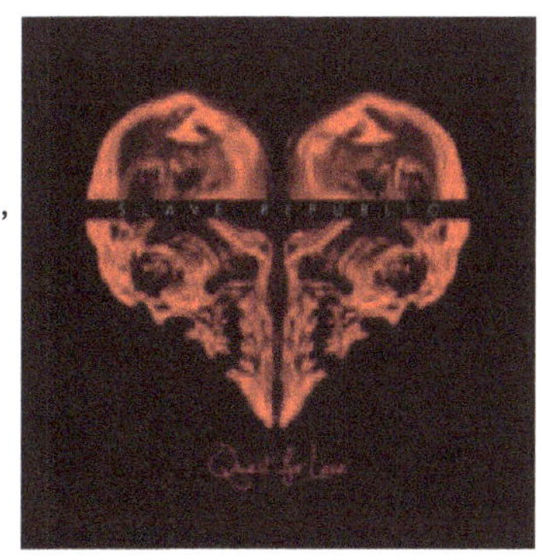

Ruined Conflict return for their second effort "Revolutionary Mayhem" in dramatic and epic style as can be expected from them. The American duo really shows a full grasp of the genre they have entered and for fans of VNV Nation you could not ask for a better band to explore. While I love all of VNV Nation's albums, Ruined Conflict has created a sound that makes me think of VNV's older days. "Revolutionary Mayhem" takes all of the dramatic and sweeping electronics of an album written about the fall of mankind in the late 90s and beefs them up for a modern take.

The most surprising fact about "Revolutionary Mayhem" to me is the lyrics. Most of these songs come across as a collection of poems written about every aspect of love. From the tenderness and dedication love can bring out of a person, to the vengeful hatred that can grow only from the purest of love becoming corrupted, the lyrics really are more impactful than most releases this year.

"Stricken" is a stunning and angry song of brutal synths and naked rage. Then "Perfection" quite honestly is brutally open and honest and vulnerable. "Legacy" is sad and hopeful but gives us their most interesting hard-hitting synths that really bring something fresh to their sound. "Weak and Impaired" is probably the most danceable, club-friendly track that sounds like someone drowned old-school electronic with brand new EBM that sings of the most hope one can dance to. With a title like "Revolutionary Mayhem," I thought I was in for more of a rise-up-and-destroy record, but I see it speaks to the mayhem within in stunning synth glory.

When Slave Republic came to the scene with their 2010 debut "Electric One" I was instantly a fan and found them interesting and engaging, I couldn't wait to see what they would do next. Three years later came "Quest For Love" and they certainly exceeded all expectations. Daniel Myer produced their sophomore release and helped elevate their sound to a whole new level. The album carries the band's 80s influenced style to a new and modern electronic realm.

Guitars perfectly accent each track to bring their vintage synth-pop sound to full realization. "Paint My Heart Black" is one of the strongest power-pop songs you'll ever hear. It's perfectly 80s with modern EBM to make something that transcends both. The vocal production is gorgeous and each sound is perfectly balanced, "Paint My Heart Black" showcases Slave Republic's maturity in design, writing and execution. Their power extends to every song in one of the most cohesive of modern albums I've come across. "Walking Ghost" brings in those light little guitar sounds akin to Depeche Mode or Iris and delivers on the promise set up by the opening track: that you're in for nostalgia updated to a whole new level of delivery. "Promises and Broken Hearts" brings a bit of Imperative Reaction style to form something more suited for club rotation.

Where Slave Republic really shines is where they deliver the beautiful and melancholic "Fall Asleep." Listening to it you could see how The Cure and Depeche Mode could overlap in each of their most beautiful styles, and Slave Republic commits to each and every component with the utmost dedication. They expertly layer a surprising amount of synth sounds in the background and showcase amazing vocals to create a flawless and fully-realized style.

JESUS AND THE GURUS
BLOOD SWEAT & TEARS

Label: Black Rain
2008
Electronic-Industrial

by Sergio Manghina

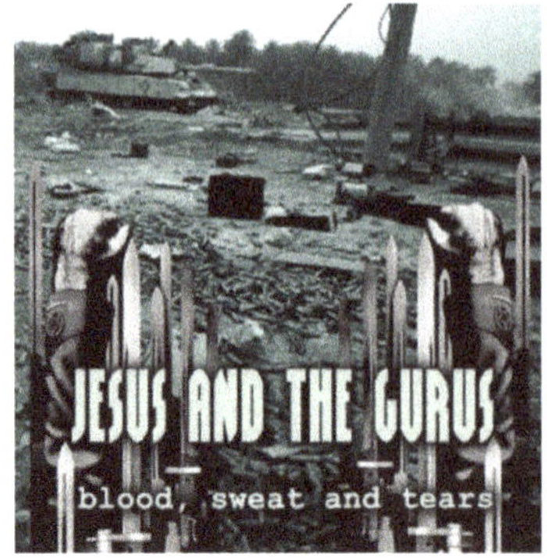

SCHNEEWITTCHEN
PERLEN VOR DIE SAUEN

Label: Danse Macabre
2008
Electro-Gothic

by Sergio Manghina

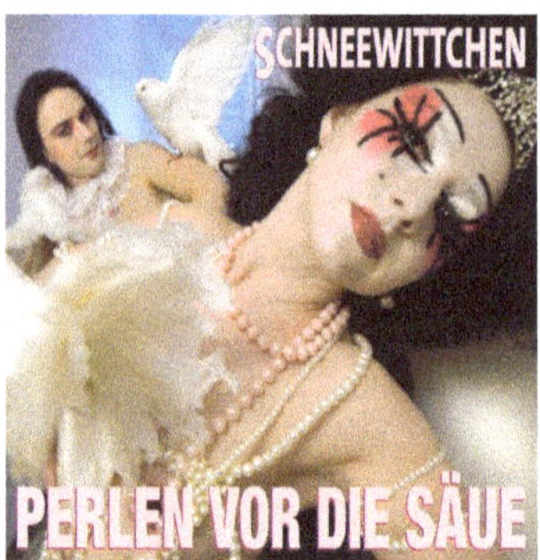

With an ultra-sharpened sound, Jesus And The Gurus have achieved a remarkable place in the European industrial scene building an iconoclastic machine against the contemporary decadence, also made of cynical lyrics and an often disturbing public image.

However, reaching their fourth album, after a long career started in 1994, this controversial Swiss band, seems always more locked inside the same nightmare, sometimes unable to enlarge its own dynamic vision, risking to be restricted between a disconforming apocalyptical gloominess and a monolithic form of industrial-metal, fortunately saved by a few excellent neo-folk episodes.

The threatening drums of "Jesus Marsch", open with a powerful marching song that emerges - solemn and stately - from a realistic and croaking old 78rpm record, melting a gentle female voice inside an impressive martial gait. This promising beginning, slips into the whirling guitar riff of "We Will Love You", a perfect metal-device, even good as a potential hit.

From this point, all the mechanism alternatively keeps ascending and descending currents and if "Eiszeit" constitutes an efficacious example of bizarre electro-industrial sing-song, "You and Me" is an original hammering lullaby, filled with some agreeable and unexpected psychedelic flavours.

"Gib mir Kraft" presents a valuable gothic keyboard-touch, able to transform - with the previous "Pride Of Switzerland" - the extreme-noise attitude into an exit door on the path of an harsh melody, settling a certain gliding fluidity.

A pleasing surprise is the final track entitled "China, China", another great marching song, that spreads eastern spices inside ear, advancing gravely and sombrely until the conclusion of the trial, like a definitive final cut.

This album by Schneewittchen is a double-faced work, containing some formidable sparks of great neo-classical goth-style, joined with a predominant attitude to dark-cabaret, as usual for this eclectic duo from Hannover, Germany.

Thomas Duda behind keyboards and Marianne Iser own a relevant talent for composing excellent melodies selecting every shade among an infinite palette of colours, one of each idea or feeling.

The first two tracks, "Komm wir ritzen us die Adern" and "Ohne Liebe" are that kind of pleasing and ultra-pop songs perfectly suitable for dancing with slow steps but completely out of context.

An ethereal theremin-sound, announces a radical change of direction to a glittering, martial electro-dance entitled "Ich war in Gold".

After the harmless "Gemeinsam untergehn", they seriously begin to show their full potential with "Sonnenuntergang" an imposing and dramatic mini-suite, splitted in two brief and distinct movements. Firstly, Marianne crosses the shadows built by a metronomic drumming, melted into a superb romantic mood, almost a solitary Marlene Dietrich walking among the ruins of a wasted town. Thereupon, while a dense and threatening sound tapestry spreads everywhere electronic beats.and ominous sirens, she sings an alienated monologue,

"Der Mann meines Lebens" is another glooming highlight, similar to a longing German lied and enriched by piano, guitar and strings. On "Rosengarten", they work around an extremely evocative piece, occasion for a further dazzling vocal performance offered by the singer, but the most remarkable songs remain "Du hast die Liebe verraten", a hypnotic and swinging dance wrapped around a beautiful mid-eastern nuance, and the nostalgic imagination of "Schwartze Madonna",

Amelie
Directed by: Jean-Pierre Jeunet
Release date: November 2, 2001

By Shahinaz Geneid

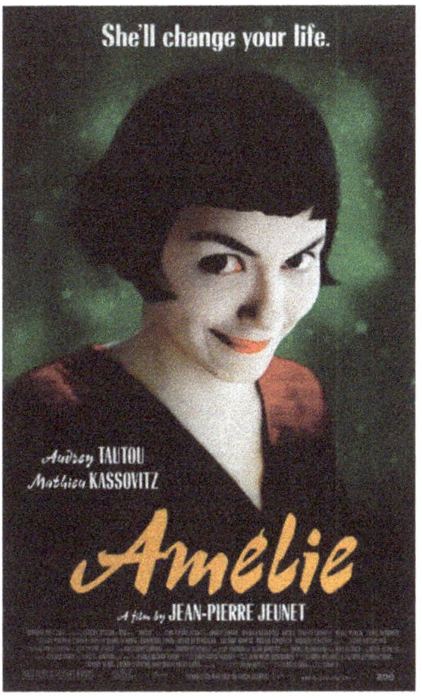

Amelie is a 2001 romantic comedy about a young, shy waitress living in Paris. She is surrounded by an eclectic cast of characters in her day to day life, and works to better the lives of these people, even in the smallest of ways. However, she, herself, is secretly incredibly lonely and isolated.

The film whimsically depicts Parisian life and Amelie's eccentric and fascinating everyday life. Her eccentric nature is largely due to her having developed an active imagination as a child when she was sequestered from other children and people by her parents. She leaves home and becomes a waitress in Montmartre, where she is shown to find contentment in being freely imaginative and enjoying the simple pleasures of life. She later on in the story decides to devote herself to bringing happiness to other people and helping the people in her daily life. Along the way, she meets Nino Quincampoix, a man who collects discarded photographs from photo booths, and begins to fall in love with him.

The film humorously explores her everyday life and her small adventures as she helps others and quickly falls passionately in love with Nino as she leads him around Paris in an attempt to get him to pursue her so that they may meet and she may return his album of discarded photographs.

Amelie is an incredibly quirky, simple, and charming love story presented in a very visually interesting and delightfully absurd cinematic style.

Blue is the Warmest Color
Directed by: Abdellatif Kechiche
Release date: October 25, 2013

By Shahinaz Geneid

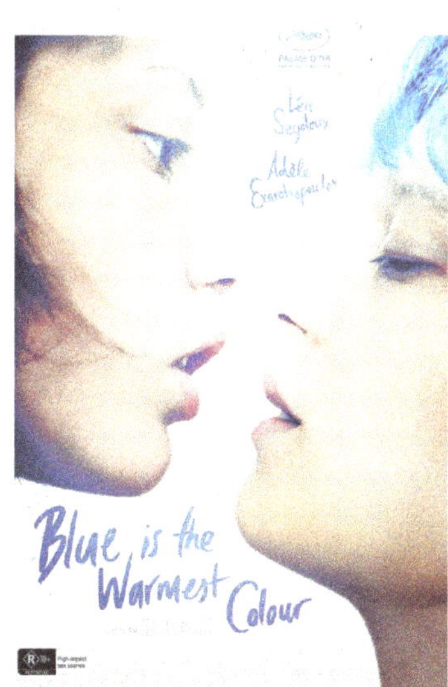

Abdellatif Kechiche's 2013 romantic drama starring Lea Seydoux and Adele Exarchopoulos is about a French teenaged girl whose life changes when she meets a strange, blue-haired woman and they fall in love. Adele, an extremely introverted teenager who dreams of becoming a teacher, begins to discover her sexuality and sense of freedom as she further pursues a relationship with Emma, the blue-haired painter whom she meets at a gay bar. The film is an ongoing celebration and exploration of the two women and their lives and loves. It portrays the youth of the current generation in all of their beauty and brightness and struggles.

The film won the Palme d'Or at the 2013 Cannes Film Festival and was nominated as the Best Foreign Language Film at the 71st Golden Globe Awards. It was lauded for boldly and transparently approaching modern issues such as sexuality, which was explored not just between its two female lead characters, but between multiple different male and female characters of various racial backgrounds and socioeconomic circumstances throughout the film. It also dealt with social, political, and economic issues of modern youth in France, presenting a broad spectrum of modern life and circumstances of young people today. Because of this, Blue is the Warmest Color was likely the best film of 2013.

Its use of symbolism and imagery is also notable and brilliantly executed. The color blue is used to represent curiosity, ecstasy, love, and more as experienced not only by Adele, but also by modern youth in general.

Overall, the film is deep, complex, and touching in its exploration of a myriad number of experiences and emotions faced by modern youth and it is an incredible visual experience.

Horror of Dracula
Director: Terrence Fisher
Distributed: Warner Bros.
Released: May 8, 1958

By Mark Hickman

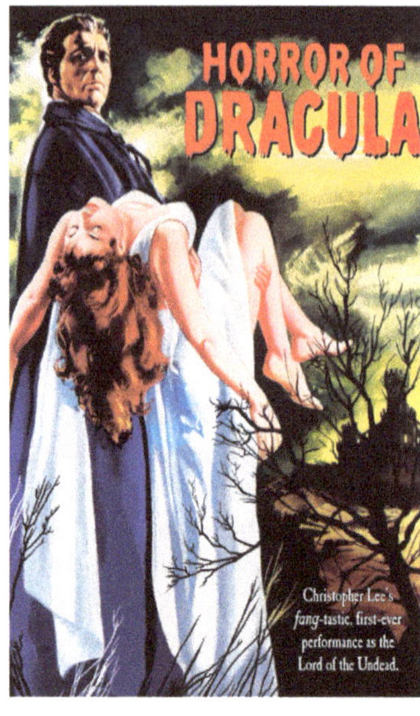

Horror of Dracula is one of the earliest films produced by Hammer studios and stars the much younger Christopher Lee in the title role, and Peter Cushing in the role of his nemesis, Van Helsing. Also, another famous cast member, Michael Gough, portrays the role of Arthur – the husband of Mina (Melissa Stribling) and father of Lucy (Carol Marsh).

After arriving at the gigantic castle of Dracula, his guest, Jonathan (John Van Eyssen), quickly discovers his true nature. After being attacked by a crazy lady and waking up the next morning to see the bite marks on his neck, he waits until near the end of day (don't ask why) to finally strike back at Dracula. Unfortunately, this assassination attempt doesn't work, and he is captured.

From this point on, the film follows Van Helsing, as he discovers Jonathan's undead body, and kills it. Now seeking a way to stop Dracula, Helsing goes on a mission to do so – and avenge the death of his friend, while preventing any more people from becoming victims.

Next to the 1931 Bela Lugosi version, this one is one of the more popular adaption's of Bram Stoker's novel. And while unfortunately we don't get to see John play the bat-crazy Jonathan Redfield in this adaption, we still get great performances from Peter and Christopher. Overall, like the Lugosi film, this is one of the most entertaining Dracula films out there.

The Mummy
Director: Terence Fisher
Distributed: Warner Bros.
Released: December 16, 1959

By Mark Hickman

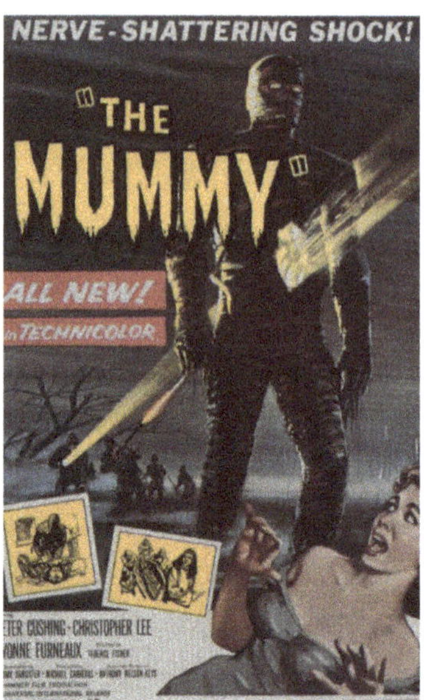

Made shortly after Horror of Dracula, The Mummy is another Hammer production that stars two cast members from the Dracula film; Peter Cushing and Christopher Lee as the undead guardian. Other stars includes; Yvonne Furneaux, George Pastell, Felix Aylmer, Raymond Huntley, and Eddie Byrne.

Within the first fourteen minutes, we are introduced to our main characters and the events that set the rest of the picture into motion. John Banning, his father, uncle, and a team of diggers discover the tomb of Karnak and briefly confront Mehemet Bay. Shortly after, John's father finds the Mummy, turning him partly crazy. Mehemet is also unhappy the tomb has been bothered and unleashes the Mummy to kill all who disturbed the tomb.

As you may know, I'm quite the fan of Peter Cushing and, like usual, he does a great job. Christopher Lee's performance as the Mummy was also surprisingly good, which is an impressive feat to do with very little dialogue for his character. The rest of the cast also did good work on their parts.

The only main criticism I have with this film is nothing specific to it, but aimed at the general lore the Mummy movies follow, which is the fact that the Mummy is rising by simply reading a piece of written text. Also, on a minor critique, the flashbacks to the beginning of the movie are inconsistent with the timing of the scenes we saw at that point.

In closing, this version of The Mummy is very entertaining and is perhaps my personal favorite version of the story.

The Perks of Being a Wallflower
Directed by: Stephen Chbosky
Release date: September 21, 2012

By Shahinaz Geneid

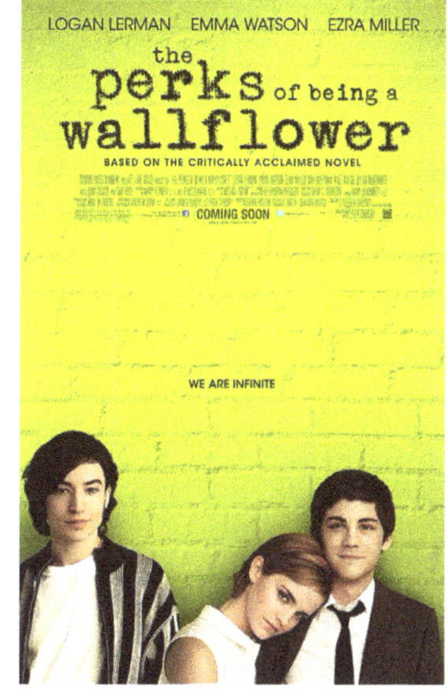

The Perks of Being a Wallflower is a 2012 coming-of-age film based on the novel by Stephen Chbosky. It explores the experience of a teenage boy beginning high school named Charlie who befriends a group of seniors.

Charlie is very shy and has difficulty making friends when he begins high school. He becomes friends with two step-siblings, Sam and Patrick, who bring him into their group of friends. The movie follows the friends during Charlie's first year and their last year of high school as they experience life, relationships, the excitement of preparing for college, the frustrations of testing, and general teenage social life. However, the film also further explores the issues of a friend's suicide and repressed sexual abuse in Charlie's life, and his struggles undergoing therapy for his issues. The film and novel are a reflection on the effects of this issues, but also a celebration of the complexities of being young and of how simple and "infinite" we can feel in some moments of our youth, also.

The Perks of Being a Wallflower is heartfelt and unpretentious in its depiction of the joys and struggles of Charlie and his friends and very much true to the essence of the original novel.

The Vampire Lovers
Director: Roy Ward Baker
Distributed: Metro-Goldwyn-Mayer
Released: 4 October 1970

By Mark Hickman

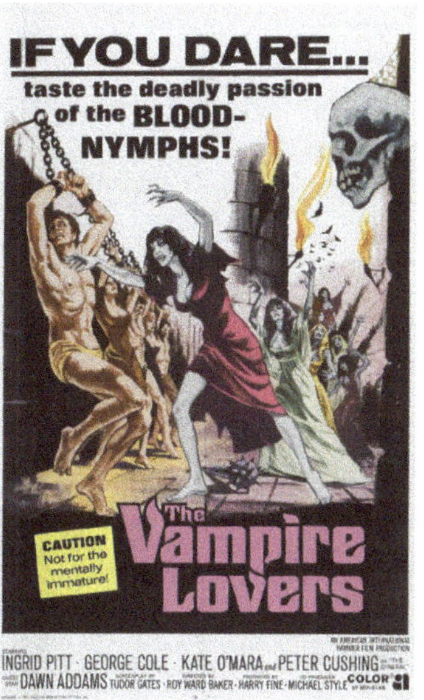

The Vampire Lovers is a Hammer-horror picture from the early 70's, and stars Ingrid Pitt as the lead vampire: Marcilla/Carmilla, Pippa Steele as Laura, Madeline Smith as Emma, and Peter Cushing in the role: General Von Spielsdorf.

The main cast all did a fine job, but for me – Ingrid and Peter are both are pretty much the highlight of the film, despite Cushing's character being present only for the first and last thirty-minutes of the movie. As for the other viewers, their highlight of the film may be the erotic scenes between Marcilla and her female victims.

The vampires in this film are done a bit differently than most I have seen. Here, they are treated as a Vampire/Ghost hybrid. In fact, the opening of the movie even features a vampire dressed in sheets. I don't know why, but I guess we can always make up something. Also, certain scenes have shots where Marcilla mysteriously disappears through doors.

The movie has plenty of erotic and gory scenes to keep some entertain, but for me personally - I only came to see Peter Cushing. Overall, The Vampire Lovers is…okay. It's not something I'm really into that much, but it's not something I hate either. If you like erotic vampire movies; then this one is something you might like to rent once just to check it out.

"Doctor Sleep" by Stephen King
Release Date: September 24th, 2013
Rating: 4 stars

By Anthony McCracken

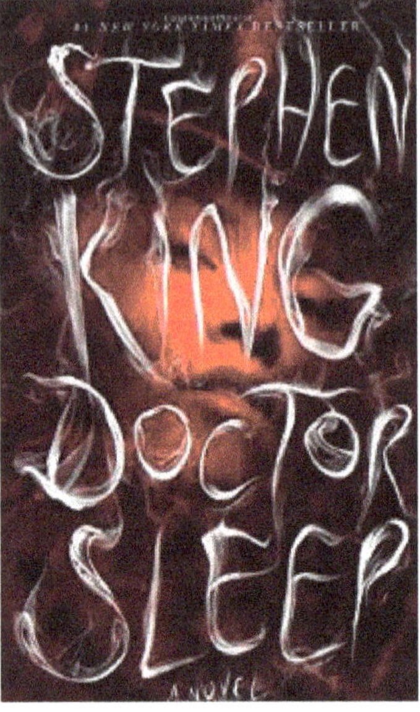

Even though it's been 36 years since "The Shining" was first published, Stephen King's "Doctor Sleep" picks up only a few years after the events of The Overlook hotel in Colorado. The prologue begins with young Danny Torrance's continued struggles with his "gift" of the shining. The novel soon fast forwards to Danny's adulthood where he has struggled to build a life of his own while purposefully dulling his gift with alcohol and in some ways following too closely in his father's footsteps.

While this sets up a sequel to "The Shining" novel, it becomes something that is entirely its own work that focuses on a new story to use Danny as a character. His teenage years are completely omitted in order to tell a story of his involvement in a larger tale involving another young person "gifted" with the shining and a travelling pack of vampiric beings that feed on the very ability Danny struggles with.

Middle-aged Danny Torrance and young Abra are very well-realized along with one of Stephen King's best villains in years. This new tale that sprawls around the United States (and even includes that infamous Colorado location) has more of a Dark Tower feel to it than a Shining feel. Some characters could have used more time, but King has made a more concise and focused novel than in recent years. Just be aware that this is a sequel to the original novel and not the Kubrick interpretation which possibly necessitates a wonderful excuse to read "The Shining" before diving in to "Doctor Sleep."

"Harrowgate" by Kate Maruyama
Year of Release: 2013

By Mario Piumetti

2013 should be called the Year of the Ghost Story, the genre getting a vibrant coat of paint. These new colors include Kate Maruyama's debut novel Harrowgate.

Michael Gould has returned home to find his wife Sarah cautious and protective of their newborn son Tim. Among them is Greta, a suspicious doula who is too domineering for Michael's tastes. Under Greta's orders, Sarah struggles to keep Michael home. A visit from her sister Anna reveals that Sarah and Tim died in Michael's absence and he realizes their ghosts haunt him. Sarah suggests they try going on like a normal couple, but with friends and relatives arriving to offer emotional support, she and Tim frequently retreat to a place called the Dark. Michael begins retaking control of his life, threatening Greta's hold over the family, but hesitates to go forward with the funeral, fearing that it will mean the end of Sarah and Tim.

Harrowgate's theme of oppressive love and the urge to hold on to the familiar keeps the Gould's together to the point where it's stifling. Maruyama makes time between the living and the dead elastic, jarring us out of our everyday experiences right from the start. Minutes that Michael spends away from home translate into weeks for the rest of the family. Readers might find Greta to be an anticlimactic villain, the confrontations between her and Michael more a battle of wills than a fight to the death, but she is merely the personification of Harrowgate's true threat of losing one's family forever.

A rewarding experience for horror fans in general, Harrowgate will surely be more so for new readers of the genre.

www.ingramcontent.com/pod-product-compliance
Lightning Source LLC
Chambersburg PA
CBHW040935070726
47599CB00037B/1873